BOOK B

BASIC READING
TEACHER'S EDITION

GLENN McCRACKEN
New Castle, Pennsylvania

CHARLES C. WALCUTT
Queens College, Flushing, New York

in collaboration with

MARY F. BOND
STATE COLLEGE AT FRAMINGHAM, FRAMINGHAM, MASSACHUSETTS

ESTHER FAIRCLOTH
MALDEN PUBLIC SCHOOLS, MALDEN, MASSACHUSETTS

J. B. LIPPINCOTT COMPANY
PHILADELPHIA, NEW YORK

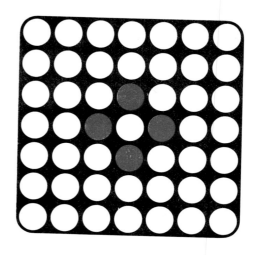

10.749.1

Contents

A MESSAGE TO THE TEACHER
FROM THE AUTHORS

What Is Reading?

At first glance, it would hardly seem worth the trouble to answer this question because, in a sense, everybody knows perfectly well what reading is. But definitions underline all intellectual enterprises, and since definitions are also assumptions, they control the activities that are based on them. Another way of saying this is that "definitions are programs": they establish the terms in which people will think about an undertaking. Until modern times, medical knowledge was controlled by the assumption that there were four "humours" (blood, phlegm, yellow bile, and black bile) which determined a person's health and temperament. With these assumptions, it was impossible for a doctor to "see" many facts that remained invisible because the theory—and especially the terminology—of humours did not permit them to exist.

Our definition of reading here is an attempt to explain the theory and practice upon which BASIC READING rests. To define reading, we must try to get at the element that sets it apart from other similar activities. It will not do, for example, to define reading as a thought-getting process, because we get thoughts just as surely from a lecture or a conversation. There is, to put it another way, no difference between "reading" a page of difficult philosophy and trying to understand it—and simply hearing the same page "read" to us by another. The problem of understanding is virtually identical for both reader and listener. So to call reading a thought-getting activity is not to identify what is particular to it.

Of course nobody would deny that the purpose of reading is to get information of some sort from the printed page. But since we get information in the same way from spoken language, this purpose does not define reading in a way that distinguishes it from listening. As soon as we grasp this point, however, the problem becomes somewhat simpler. If we see that meaning resides in language, then we can ask how writing (which we read) is related to language (which we hear and say). If language, which is sound, carries the meanings, what is writing? It seems obvious that writing is a device, a *code* if you like, for representing the sounds of language by visual forms. The written words are in fact visual symbols of the spoken words, which are sounds.

We have said that definitions, being assumptions, control the activities that are based on them. The literature on reading contains a tremendous amount of discussion on this question of the definition of itself. The richness and variety of this discussion springs from the fact that the whole field of reading theory and practice has been in a healthy state of experiment and change for many years. The debate over the definition of reading reflects this vitality.

It seems, therefore, appropriate to offer here a comprehensive definition that will not only guide and satisfy those who are using these textbooks, but will also show where our undertaking stands in relation to the whole picture of reading theory and practice today.

The problem of definition derives from the fact that the word reading has a good many meanings, several of which are involved when we speak of reading instruction in the primary grades.* The word means *pronounce, interpret, hear, search, apprehend, say aloud, study, discover the true nature of, assume a meaning, learn, gain information, have a specific wording,* and *have a certain quality*—and this list is very far from exhaustive.

We propose that reading, as we commonly use the word in connection with teaching children, beginning at about age six, has three meanings simultaneously. These meanings do not exclude one another, but rather must be seen as coexisting in the word if we are to enjoy a satisfying and productive use of it. We will identify these meanings as *reading*[1], *reading*[2], and *reading*[3], as the linguists and semanticists use these indices. Let us consider them in the order in which they grow, but always with the understanding that no one of them explains what we are doing when we teach a child to read.

The surprising and interesting thing is how different the three meanings are.

Reading[1] is decoding the printed visual symbols into the spoken sounds that they designate. Reading, in other words, is turning writing into language. Language, as all the linguistics experts assure us, is spoken sound. Writing is a visual symbolization of those sounds, just as a musical score is a visual representation of the sounds of music. Reading converts writing into language, just as a pianist converts a score into music. It is symbol into sound in both instances, the former made with the mouth and vocal apparatus, the latter with fingers on a keyboard. This definition of the first meaning of reading holds whether or not the spoken sound is understood, and it holds at both ends of a great scale. For example, at one end we can read a passage from a difficult poem without understanding it. At the other end of this scale, a child can read a single word like *fid* without understanding it. In both cases, we are converting printed symbols into proper sounds. We are turning writing into language. The parallel with music holds here too. A person might tap out the notes of a complex sonata without either grasping or reproducing the meaning of the piece; yet striking the right notes is the first and essential step toward rendering and interpreting the musical score.

Reading[2] is, strangely enough, not really reading at all! It is *understanding language,* yet it is the goal that we demand immediately upon the mastery of *reading*[1]. The distinction may be clarified with an illustration. Suppose we read aloud to you the most difficult of Shakespeare's sonnets. Suppose, for the sake of our argument, that you do not understand it. Is anything the matter with your reading? Obviously not, for you are not reading, but listening. Your problem is a problem of understanding

* Chapter 3 in Walcutt, Lamport, McCracken, *Teaching Reading: A Phonic/Linguistic Approach to Developmental Reading,* New York: Macmillan, 1974.

language. But now, and more important, suppose that we who have read the sonnet to you do not understand it either. Would you say that anything was the matter with our reading? You might, but on reflection you would have to admit that our difficulty was exactly the same as yours—a difficulty with the language. You certainly would not send us to a remedial reading teacher, but to an expert on Shakespeare. So what we call reading here is actually *understanding language*. It is *reading*[2]. We certainly have it in mind when we speak of reading. It is the element of communication that is the goal of any reading instruction, but it is the same process that applies in spoken discourse and communication.

Reading[3] is hardest to define, but essential to our use of the word. On a higher level, reading takes us into a world of art and intellect that is accessible only through the printed page. Whether history, anthropology, poetry, fiction, or philosophy is involved, we move into worlds of written discourse that are not accessible, and indeed do not exist, in spoken language. The literary style that is an essential form of the highest human thought depends on writing. We do not find the same style, the same quality of language, the same discrimination and breadth of vocabulary in spoken discourse. Where these higher qualities have appeared in spoken discourse, they have appeared there as a consequence of having been developed in writing. The intricate form of a sonnet or a Spenserian stanza, the elaborate balance of a sentence by Macaulay or Gibbon, the close structure of an essay by John Stuart Mill (a hundred other examples would do as well) have all been developed through the written language, which permits the kind of study, elaboration, and accuracy that probably could not be sustained with only a spoken language.

It is true that the epic and the ballad seem to have been developed orally. They were composed, performed, and transmitted by professional minstrels, it appears, and constitute special cases. During most periods of the historical past, it has been a commonplace that access to learning—which meant writing—brought special privileges of culture and power. The House of Intellect, which is the accumulated culture of man—which in other words is the Mind of the past brought up to and poured into the Mind of the present—has been both wrought and stored in the written word. The realms of gold, the hoardings of the world's great books, exist only in books and by virtue of the art of writing. *Reading*[3] takes us into these realms of gold, which are the reward of reading.

The first steps into *reading*[3] come as early as the child begins to read a language that he does not hear spoken. As early as third grade, surely, and often in the second the child who has learned to read will be coming upon hundreds of words that he does not say or hear, words that become part of his reading vocabulary—and these are found in sentences of a style and a precision that he will rarely hear spoken. Together, the rich precise literary vocabulary and the sentences and paragraphs of skilled writing carry a level of art and thought that rises above—though it rests upon—the very summit of spoken discourse.

The specialists in linguistics emphasize the fact that language is spoken sound and that a particular language is to be known through its spoken patterns. These are what linguistic anthropologists record with special symbols in the remotest villages, say, of Africa. It is the spoken language, furthermore, that finally seems to determine usage: a language grows in speech. We accept these considerations, but we also affirm that there are, indeed, two languages—the spoken language and the written language—and that we learn to read in order to read the written language.

There is no particular value to having first- or second-grade readers in the spoken language—that is, using only the vocabulary and the sentence structures that a first- or second-grade child would *himself* use. Reading takes the child into a different world, and this world is different precisely because it is the magical world of the written language.

And now another point that this definition clarifies: reading instruction that begins with a sight vocabulary skips over *reading*[1] and goes on to *reading*[2], with the special complication that it attaches meaning directly to the printed symbol. Such instruction treats printing, that is, as if it were language. A sight word is taught first as a meaning rather than as a symbol of a sound. Using context and picture clues, the child is led to reason and guess what a word may mean, rather than to figure out what sound that printed word represents and then go on to refer the sound to his knowledge of language. Under this approach, reading is defined as "bringing meaning to the printed page," and the definition clearly reveals that the child is being led to *deduce* the meaning of a printed word in a sentence rather than to *decode* that printed word into its proper sound and then *understand the language* that he has unlocked.

Parallels with music flood over us at this point. The virtuoso pianist pours out his interpretation without any thought about individual notes or scales, yet he had to learn those notes and scales with painstaking repetition and practice before he could be liberated from them. So with reading. The more carefully and accurately the mechanical skill of decoding the print into sound is mastered, the sooner it can be forgotten in the delight of accurate reading for meaning and enjoyment. Fortunately, the skill of reading is a great deal easier to learn than playing the piano.

Theory and Practice

Now, what is the value of our definition as regards the teaching of reading? We believe its value is that it enables us to put first things first and approach the task of learning to read, with our children, in an orderly and effective manner. We are intensely concerned that our children understand what they read, but the "decoding" skill must come first if we are to get them started properly.

For the truth is that the language, the imagination, the experience, and the conversation of a typical six-year-old child are enormously far beyond anything he is going to be able to read for some time. It will be quite a few months before anything he can read will even approach the vocabulary and thought of what he has heard or even spoken himself. We believe this is more true today than it was in the past. What the child hears on radio or television is often very advanced linguistically compared to what he will read in his first books.

So the faster we teach him the skill, the faster will his ability to read catch up with his language, which, of course, has had a six-year head-start. Once he has mastered the skill, this relation changes radically: reading[3] becomes the prime source of growth in vocabulary, in language, and in intellect. Within a very few years the child who has learned to read properly will be reading and understanding hundreds of words that he may not regularly speak or hear until he is attending college!

In view of these facts, we do not hesitate to say that the rewards of the first steps in reading are not impressive growth in experience or vocabulary. There are rewards, however, of two sorts. First, there is the great satisfaction of mastering a skill in an orderly fashion. If an analogy will help here, we might say that first steps in reading are like first steps in learning to drive an automobile. Both skills have enormous attractions to the young learner, for they are gateways to many joys. The learning car-driver has these rewards in mind, but at the start he is totally engrossed simply in the activity of learning to drive. At this stage he has no thought of going anywhere; learning to operate the automobile is reward and interest enough in itself. And so it is with reading. The reward of emulating the grownups, for whom reading is obviously very important, is the long-range goal; but the skill itself is reward and delight for the beginner.

On top of this delight in learning for itself, we seek to reward the young learner with amusing or exciting stories as fast as we have the words for them; and in fact we accumulate vocabulary very much more rapidly than has been done with the standard basal readers in recent years. Yet, even though this program accumulates a vocabulary well in excess of 2,000 words in the first grade (as contrasted with as few as 325 words in standard basal readers) and proceeds in a similar fashion in subsequent grades, the teacher will be surprised to discover how very elementary it is and how very far beneath the actual speaking and hearing vocabularies of her pupils it is.

The pleasure and confidence of the child are reinforced by the outstanding feature of this program: With the exception of a handful of special words (only 2 in *Book A*) every story contains only the letter-sounds that have been taught at any point. No letter or spelling appears until after the lesson in which it is presented.

Some Linguistic Aspects of Reading

At this point we should like to make it clear that BASIC READING offers more than many of the new so-called linguistic systems of reading instruction. It uses various principles that have been strongly and properly emphasized by the linguistics specialists. But it also incorporates many of the best characteristics of the standard basal systems; and it has an entirely new system of presenting letters, sound-spellings, words, and sentences in a *coherent* and *integrated* pattern. This latter, as we shall explain, is what sets it apart from other reading programs.

On the question of beginning instruction with *reading*[1], however, we are in total accord with the best linguistic thinking, which declares that "language is spoken sound" and that reading instruction must first establish the relations between the spoken sounds and the letters that spell them. As you know, this position has been challenged since the early 1920's by those who believe that reading should begin with experience charts, paragraphs, sentences, and whole words. The argument *against* beginning with sounds and letters is too complex for us to answer in full. We should, rather, prefer to dispose of it as simply as possible. Let us just touch on what may seem to be the strongest point—that much English spelling is so irregular, so "un-phonic," that it defies a systematic approach. Sharply aware of this condition, we begin with the most regular spellings, the short vowels and the sounded consonants, and with these alone we accumulate vocabulary very quickly and use it in meaningful sentences and stories. We do not stress spelling patterns to the point of monotony or absurdity. Let us illustrate with three examples: In "Oh! oh! Look, look, something!" we have very common words with very irregular, un-simple spellings. In "Pat can bat at a fat cat," we have highly consistent spelling patterns without much sense in the sentence. In our system you may find a sentence like "Dan bent his dad's fender," which is made of three short vowels and only eight sounded consonants—and makes sense as a sentence. Here, then, we combine the virtues of basal readers and linguistic principles without the shortcomings of either.

Now, to answer further the argument against beginning with sounds and letters, we offer what may at first glance seem to be a startling contradiction: We contend that the irregular spelling of so many common words constitutes the strongest argument for beginning with the regular elements of English spelling. Why? Simply because if our spelling system is approximately 85 per cent regular, it would seem proper to begin with the regular system before taking up the exceptions. This is the heart of our method. We find that when the child learns, at the beginning, one consistent thing after another, he rapidly gains understanding and confidence. There are no mysterious configurations that he must memorize without clues, so that he may confuse words like **after** and **alter,** or even little words like **then** and **always.** Rather, he learns why and how the letters represent the sounds of the word. With this clue, his learning is vastly simplified and accelerated. Our aim is to make him recognize words instantly, and we find that he does this with the least drill when he knows why the letters that make up a certain word are there. If we give him a dozen sight words, he may confuse **then** and **always** because he knows them only as pure configurations; but when he knows the letters first, he understands why these letters spell the sound of the word, and his recognition of the *whole word* at a glance (which is the goal of *any* reading system) is easier for him than it would have been if he had learned the same word only as a whole, without benefit of accompanying training in letters.

At this point we should like to refine our definition of *reading*[1] with a further thought. If learning language is learning the meanings of sounds (i.e., words), learning *reading*[1] is *learning letter significance,* for the entire system of alphabetic writing is based on the use of letters to indicate individual sounds. The phoneme-grapheme (i.e. sound-spelling) relations in English orthography seem very imperfect when we look at strange spellings like **might, cough, should, colonel, sleigh,** and **machine.** And indeed English orthography is needlessly bad, for we use 26 letters to spell 44 basic phonemes in more than 250 different ways. That is one side of the matter; but if we look at all the words that are spelled regularly, and then set about organizing the irregular spellings into minor groups and patterns, we find that it is not an impossible accomplishment. And if we begin with the regular system, it is not at all difficult to master the exceptions when they are taken up, later, one group at a time.

Sound and Sense: Basic Letter Knowledge with No "Sounding Out"

Many teachers wonder whether the mechanical process of "sounding out" a strange word will not interfere with a child's ability to attend to its meaning. They know that a child may have trouble putting two isolated sounds together, and they fear that the struggle to do so may drive all thought of meaning out of his mind. This could be a real problem. A child may have the greatest difficulty looking at letters individually and then trying to say-them-together into a syllable or word. We have solved this problem by virtually eliminating the laborious pronouncing and combining of isolated sounds.

Impossible?

Not at all. Indeed, very simple. It is merely a question of method.

Let us begin with the solid assumption that the child hears and says thousands of words just about as well as we do. So he knows the sounds-combined that are words. Our task is to help him hear the phonemes in the words that he hears and says very well. He says "fat" perfectly. Beginning there, we get him to recognize, to identify its three sounds. At the same time we show him how the three letters represent these sounds. This can all be done without any sounding-out at all: we begin with the whole word, identify its phonemes, and then connect those sounds with their spellings.

As you will see in the detailed instructions in this manual, we first demonstrate to the child how the two letter-sounds of **a** and **n** are brought together to make the word **an.** Thereafter, with every letter presented we make new words; but instead of asking the child to gasp the letters together into a word, we consistently show him how the phoneme-grapheme relationships appear in the new words. This is effectively done through demonstration by the teacher. Having taught **a, n,** and then **r,** we demonstrate **r-a-n** . . . **ran** by showing how the sounds occur in the word. To put it another way, we teach the words as wholes while we lead the child to see how the sounds that he knows occur in each word and are systematically represented by the letters in it.

This procedure is *apparently* so little different from the customary method of getting the child to fuse cuh-aaa-tuh into **cat,** yet it is so completely different in theory and result that we should like to develop it here in more detail. Let us look at our particular emphasis in the light of some recent scholarship. Remember, we recommend 1) hearing the whole word, 2) identifying its phonemes, and 3) THEN learning how the letters "picture" those sounds.

Assuming the opposite approach, the distinguished Russian professor, D. B. Elkonin, writing in *Comparative Reading,* edited by John Downing (New York: Macmillan, 1973), discusses as *The Riddle of the Reading Process* the fact that even when children know their letters and the sounds they represent, they are very frequently not able to sound out a new syllable correctly:

> "Even if the child has learned the alphabetic characters and their sounds, he is not able to create from them the sound form of a word or a syllable. Why is it that a child who knows the characters and their sounds still cannot read the word or syllable they compose? This, strictly speaking, is the riddle of the reading process . . . One could demonstrate that the entire history of methods of teaching reading is one of hypotheses about this riddle." (Page 571.)

What this boils down to is the fact that a child can know the sounds of his letters *in isolation* and yet not be able to sound out a new syllable or word. Professor Elkonin explains why it is so difficult for children to sound out new words. It is because the second letter often affects the pronunciation of the first one. The sound represented by a letter is different in different positions. Thus there are a great many "versions of phonemes," as they are called. The same letter sounds different in different positions, but in a word we know, we make the right sound naturally. When we know the words as wholes we don't even hear the differences in these sounds.

But these little differences are what make it difficult to sound out an unfamiliar word. When the child is asked to sound letters together to produce a word he has not "read" before, he does not know what he is working toward, and he frequently cannot make his way from the first sound to the second. Versions of phonemes (technically "allophones") are the different sounds of **t** in these words: **toe, stow, tree, hatpin, catcall, cats, catnip, button, metal,** and **city.** To the good adult reader, these **t**'s all sound alike, because he does not need to hear their differences or think about them. But if one were trying to sound out these words correctly, *not having heard them before,* he would have great difficulty making the correct sound for each **t.**

This is why we put such great stress on 1) beginning with the whole word, 2) hearing its sounds (its phonemes), and 3) THEN connecting the sounds with the letters that spell them. This approach solves "The riddle of the reading process."

Our explanation immediately raises a question. It is, "That's all very well for the first steps, but do you plan to teach the child every word he

xii

ever learns to read in this manner? If so, how will he ever become an independent reader?" The answer is important. It is that by the method we propose the child quickly comes into possession of a store of syllables and letter-clusters, such as **spl, spr, ick, tch, ult, alt, str,** and **ing,** that reliably and consistently represent sounds wherever they occur. It is with these that he "attacks" a new word, and this method is just what a good adult reader uses. We know the syllables and clusters, and we use them as our units-of-attack for new words. The best research we know indicates that good young readers attack new words with these weapons. They do not sound out a-letter-at-a-time.

With respect to these clusters, we should like to make a further point: A child can hear and distinguish the two phonemes in **sm** as easily as he can hear and distinguish the two phonemes in **is.** It is as easy for him to hear a consonant phoneme as a vowel phoneme. This brings us to the question of letter order.

Letter Order

Why our particular letter order? We introduce the five short vowels in *Book A* because they permit the construction of short words free from such complexities as digraphs (**ea, ee, ei, ai, ay,** etc.) and the silent or signal **e** of such words as **late.** Every word has a vowel; so they are particularly useful and needed. We follow the first vowel (**a**) with a consonant (**n**) so that we can immediately have a word to work with, in the manner we have set forth. With the second consonant (**r**), we have four words and a little story; and the third consonant gives us four more words. The last of these is **and,** with the first blend. Since, as we have said, a child can hear a blend as easily as a syllable, we do not approach blends as special problems or as items that have to be presented individually *as* blends.

It will also be noted that the first two consonants are *fricatives* or *continuants,* rather than *plosives.* Their sounds can be sustained indefinitely, just like a vowel sound. One can draw out n-n-n-n-n or r-r-r-r-r as long as his breath lasts. Plosives, like **d** and **p,** demand a sudden opening of the breathstream and so cannot be sustained. For the very first words the continuants make it possible for the teacher to demonstrate more easily, i.e. run the sounds of aaaaa-nnnnn together. The teacher can do the same with Nnnnnn-aaaaa-nnnnn, making the word with a continuing sound. The elements can be made longer or shorter, until the children understand that the word is composed of two sounds, or three sounds. **Ran** has three sounds, all of which can be sustained in pronunciation.

After two continuants, the secret will have been grasped, and we go on to the plosive **d.** By page 12, we have added **u, m,** and **p,** and we have made *twenty-six* regularly-spelled words. The *essence of reading* can be learned with these first seven letters. Indeed, it can be grasped with the first three or four. So here is where to take your time and get a solid start. We proceed with the most frequent consonants, saving **q, x,** and **z** until much later—they come after **sh, wh,** and **th.**

Thus we begin with simple spellings in simple, familiar words. All the sounds are on the whole equally easy for a typical child; he knows them all and has known them for years. We want to begin with simple words that are simply *spelled*. Instead of vocabulary control in terms of word frequency, we use phoneme-grapheme (i.e. sound-spelling) control in terms of simplicity and regularity—moving into the irregular spellings after the regular ones have been mastered.

You will see, as you work with the system, that the steady accumulation of new words, first in lists and then in stories (which, let us emphasize again, use only the letter-sounds that have been taught up to any point), comes as the child learns to recognize letter-sounds in words. He gets the word as a whole while he recognizes the letter elements that spell it on the page.

This procedure not only avoids the dangers inherent in labored sounding out, but also from the very beginning teaches the children to see words as wholes. The whole sound-spelling pattern and the whole meaning pattern are joined into a single unit of perception. This is another way of saying that we want every word the child learns to become a "sight" word for him, in the sense that he recognizes it instantly as a whole. This goal is tremendously simplified and expedited if the child, while seeing the word as a whole, also knows the letters that make it and knows why those particular letters make it. He need not pronounce the word either aloud or to himself, but he recognizes the printed word as a systematic representation of the spoken word—because he knows the system.

In short, following this program the child learns from the beginning to see words exactly as the most skillful adult readers see them: not as configurations or silhouettes, but as whole images of complete words with all their letters. We have these images—of thousands and thousands of words—already in our minds, and it is these perfect images of the whole words that we see as we read rapidly. So remarkable is the trigger-mechanism of the brain that a good reader, going at top speed, will actually see *answer* when the word on the page is misprinted as *ansmer*. What clues the human perceptive apparatus uses in perceiving words so rapidly is still a mystery.

We should like to take this occasion to clear up a myth about reading that recurs with surprising frequency. It is that the people who believe in a phonic-linguistic approach teach what is termed "word calling" and do not care about "reading for meaning." If we stress sound-spelling relationships, it is precisely because we are deeply concerned to cut the most direct and reliable path to meaning. As we have said earlier, printing is a visual means of representing the sounds which are language. Meaning is in these sounds. We want to equip the child to turn the written word into a spoken word (whether he actually utters it or not) so he will hear what it says, that is, get its meaning. If a child looks at a picture or thinks about the context—and then says "dish" when the printed word is "bowl," he is not reading for meaning: he is guessing. And guessing is not good enough.

xiv

Furthermore, in all our experience we have never found anybody who did not think that the purpose of reading was to get the meaning. The only possible defense of skipping sound and going directly from print to meaning would be that printed words are directly meaningful—that the printed word *green* means the color, but this is not so. It is the spoken word *green* that designates the color, while the printed word designates the sound of the spoken word. Linguistic specialists have been stressing this fact for the past two decades.

Some of the Less Obvious Aspects of Our Phonic-Linguistic System

People continually ask questions about the phonic-linguistic system of BASIC READING—questions which reveal that many teachers would like to know about some of the planning that went into its formulation. By phonetics we mean precisely the *sounds* of the English language. These sounds existed for thousands of years before there was any writing or spelling. When the system of writing with an alphabet was invented (and this was long before the English language had evolved from its distant Indo-European roots), it could only have made possible an approximate representation of the enormous variety of speech sounds in any language.

We can illustrate this point by jumping ahead into a current example: the sound represented by the spelling **to** varies from the complete pronunciation that one might give if dictating the word for a spelling lesson, to the barest and almost inaudible **t** that we sense rather than hear when one says rapidly, "I'm going down to the store before it closes." Or consider the word "the" as it might be dictated for a spelling lesson, ending in a clear long **e**, against the same word in the middle of a sentence, where it comes out as a barely-heard **th.** When we add to these differences caused by emphasis and intonation in a sentence, the differences among allophones, or versions of phonemes, we double or triple the number of sounds that a letter may represent.

Thousands of such variations in speech sounds have never been represented by any alphabetic spelling, in whatever language. Now if we consider the fact that our alphabet was invented for an earlier and different language from English, plus the fact that both the sounds and the spellings of English have evolved enormously during the past thousand years, plus the further fact that these two—the evolution of English sounds and the evolution of English spelling—have not by any means been consistently geared to each other, we can understand that our spelling renders only an approximation of our language sounds. But perhaps more surprising, on first thought, is the fact that this inaccuracy, this approximateness, is tremendously valuable. It is what makes writing possible! A Maine Yankee and a Southerner from deepest Georgia can both read a novel written in eighteenth-century England by someone who pronounced the language very differently from either of them. If the spelling represented the sounds more exactly, this would not be possible.

The Maine Yankee can write a letter to his cousin in Georgia, further-more, and be easily understood precisely *because* his spelling only approxi-mately indicates his speech sounds. A moment's reflection tells us that we all, without even thinking about it, make the adjustment between the way a sentence is spelled out in writing and the way we ourselves say it.

Children learning to read are constantly making the same sorts of ad-justments, which they make with very little instruction. They have been speaking for years before they began reading, and speech was as "natural" to them as walking. Because speech is "natural," we do not even think about a great many of the sounds that we hear and pronounce. If you ask twenty people at random whether they know that the initial sounds of **thin** and **then** are different sounds, most of them will tell you that they never thought of it. We spell the two different sounds **th** and adjust to the correct pronunciation—most of us—without realizing that there are two different sounds! Now for an amusing variation, let us consider the fact that the difference between initial **th** in **thin** and **then** is *exactly* the same kind of difference as that between the initial sounds of **fin** and **van**—which we spell with different letters. The first is "unvoiced," the second "voiced," which is all the difference. Probably not more than one person in fifty is aware of this fact—or of the same relation between **p** and **b** and between **s** and **z** and between **k** and **g**. In some cases we spell the sounds with different letters, and in some cases with the same letters. This is a complex and inconsistent procedure, but we get along very well with it; and indeed we get along very well, most of us, totally ignorant of the existence of such intricacies.

Our point is that the child learning to **read** is dealing with a system of writing that only approximates an accurate representation of the sounds. The child's guide and resource is his own speaking and hearing knowledge of the language. He identifies the written word, an imperfect symbol, with his own long and deeply established speaking knowledge of that word. He connects the **s** in **saw** with its sound, and then he con-nects the **s** in **was** with its different sound (it's a **z** in **was**, of course)— and the words come so naturally to him that he may not even realize that different sounds are represented by the **s**.

This explains why, relying on the child's own language knowledge, we have in BASIC READING not emphasized many phonetic complexities that the child does not have to be bothered with while he is learning to read. If he says varying sounds so naturally that he is unaware of their difference, so much the better for him! A trained linguist can explain that the **a** of **came** is a different sound from the **a** of **care**. We present the two words in nearby lessons without any notice of the difference, because the child does not need to be bothered with it. Few people have noticed that the **n** in **band** represents a very different sound from the **n** in **bank**. We present the **nd** in *Book A* and **nk** in *Book B*, but the latter is de-ferred only because the **k** comes in *Book B* in our sound-spelling sequence. No attention at all need be given to the fact that these are different **n** sounds, because every child says and hears them correctly. The **n** in **bank** is the same sound that is spelled **ng** in **sing**, which comes in *Book C*, but of course no special notice need be made of this fact.

xvi

Thus, what may seem to be oversights in BASIC READING are in fact carefully planned simplifications that make it easier for the child to learn to read. The professional linguistics scholar may delight in explaining the difference between the **a** in **came** and the **a** in **care**—but no child should be unduly concerned with it. It is more of a problem for college-level phonetics or linguistics.

Some Special Aspects of the Program

Readiness

A special aspect of this program is the "Accompanying Readiness," or "Functional Readiness," which teaches the readiness skills at the same time that the child is learning the names, and shapes of the first letters. This new approach to readiness is a tremendous time-saver. The pupil actually learns to read in the few weeks formerly devoted entirely to readiness. The teacher using this manual will see how naturally the two experiences go together. There is also an advantage in flexibility: the readiness exercises may be omitted whenever they are no longer needed.

Eighteen of the usual readiness skills developed at the first-grade level are "built in" the first twenty pages of *Book A*. Skills suggested in the lesson plans for these pages include:

1. Recognition of colors
2. Left-to-right eye movement
3. Recognition of similarities and differences
4. Spatial relationships
5. Concepts of *more, less,* and *fewer*
6. Following sequence of events to tell a story
7. Awareness of page numbers
8. Counting
9. Recognition of position relationships
10. Oral expression
11. Recalling details to relate a story
12. Awareness of differences in shapes
13. Line-to-line sequence
14. Interpretation of a picture story
15. Making inferences
16. Understanding of ordinals (1-6)
17. Auditory discrimination
18. Association and recognition of upper and lower case letters

The Teacher's Edition presents a suggested procedure for developing the readiness skills with the class, and there are pages in the *Book A* Workbook that serve the same end.

Special Words

The term **special** is used to designate the handful of words that are presented before their linguistic elements have been taught. These special words are necessary in order to write story material. Some words have high use value such as **said** and **for**. Others, such as **carrier** and **deliver,** are required by the content of a particular story.

In *Book A* only two special words of high use are included: **a** and **the**. *Book B* includes sixteen special words, and *Book C* contains twelve. There are no special words in *Book D*.

Consideration for Learners of Varying Abilities

It has been said of most basic reading programs that the material presented was either too much of a load for the slower learner or not challenging enough for the child blessed with exceptional ability. This program has been designed with children of various abilities in mind. In teaching the 44 sounds and presenting more than 2,000 words at the Grade One level, we present adequate material to keep the bright pupil well occupied. But the slower learning pupil need not study and master every one of the words that appear in the word lists because not all these words are necessary for successful reading of the accompanying stories. The pupils work with the word lists until they become familiar with the phoneme-grapheme relationships involved and can recognize them in new or unfamiliar words.

Book E, the first level of the Grade Two program, reviews in the same sequence, but in larger units, all the sound-spellings developed in the Grade One program. A pupil who has not completed all of *Book D* of the Grade One program need not, therefore, go back to complete it; but he can begin *Book E,* proceeding at a comfortable pace.

Workbooks, duplicating masters, and textfilms, all of which will be discussed later, provide additional tools for working with pupils of varying abilities.

The Use of the Workbooks

Workbooks, properly used, can become a valuable part of a complete developmental reading program. The activities in the BASIC READING Workbooks are designed to be done in the time allotted for reading instruction. They are not designed merely to keep the child occupied while the teacher does something else. Each exercise reinforces or develops an essential reading skill.

The workbook should be the culminating activity for each lesson. This does not mean that there must be a workbook exercise every day. At the bottom of every workbook page is a note to the teacher explaining the purpose of the page and telling what lesson in the text it follows. The Teacher's Editions for the student textbooks also contain similar instructions for correlation.

Beginning with the *Book C* Workbook, directions for use appear at the top of each page. They are placed there so that the teacher can ask her group to read them silently before calling on a single child to read them aloud and then discussing the procedures involved until they are understood by everyone. A child working on an exercise he does not understand is, of course, wasting his time. Most teachers find it desirable to do the first part of an exercise with the group, before leaving them to work by themselves. The workbooks serve the triple function of teaching, practice, and review. The more carefully an exercise is launched, with explanation and demonstration, the more it will accomplish for the child.

After they have finished an exercise, children enjoy reading some of their answers aloud. The teacher may add to this "refreshment" by sending a pupil or two to the chalkboard to write some of the important words they have been learning.

After this, it is desirable to check the workbook lessons immediately—and best of all, we think, to have each pupil correct his answers before the teacher collects the workbooks for her own examination of them.

The Use of Duplicating Masters

Duplicating masters, also properly used, can serve as a valuable adjunct to an effective reading program. A box of duplicating masters has been prepared for each of the books in the primary (Grades One-Three) program. In certain cases, these duplicating masters duplicate teaching suggestions in the Teacher's Editions, freeing the teacher from the time-consuming process of creating her own masters for reproduction. The general instructions for effective use of workbooks, previously mentioned, are appropriate for the duplicating masters.

The Use of the Textfilms

Textfilms were prepared especially to accompany and augment the BASIC READING series. Throughout the three primary-grade levels, there is at least one filmstrip frame to accompany each lesson in the program. The teacher will thus have carefully-correlated projected images to improve the teaching of every reading skill during the entire school year.

In most instances the filmstrip frames teach the same lessons as those they accompany in the textbooks, except that the film lessons are greatly condensed. This plan affords the teacher opportunities to use the film frames for introducing lessons and clarifying meanings before transferring to the textbook lessons, where she may extend the teaching and test the learning.

Careful classroom testing over a period of several years has proved this type of textfilm to be effective for various reasons:

1. For motivation of pupil interest, film can seldom be surpassed as an effective teaching tool. Attention spans are greatly lengthened. It is not unusual for a Grade-One teacher to hold the undivided attention of an entire class for as long as forty minutes while teacher and pupils work at a screen on just one image. Interest is a basic prerequisite to reading success. These textfilms will stimulate pupils' interest and curiosity so that the teacher will enjoy an ideal learning situation.

2. The textfilm provides an excellent medium for introducing new material vividly and clearly so that children can understand meanings and follow directions.

3. These textfilms provide a useful and convenient method for reviewing and testing material already taught in the textbook lessons. They are particularly helpful for this purpose because the material is greatly condensed in the films. Reviewing and testing of lessons may be accomplished in less time than would otherwise be required.
4. The film image is large and colorful, and it appears at the front of the classroom where it is readily viewed by every pupil. All the children in the room may participate in each lesson.
5. Class managament is thus simplified while textfilm frames are being projected because the children are all attentive to what is going on at the screen.
6. Film complements and reinforces other teaching techniques. It is a vivid, stimulating, clarifying, and concrete approach. This type of presentation has proved most successful with the slower learner.

A decision you will be making as you plan to teach reading with the BASIC READING series with textfilms is whether you will group your children into ability sections for initial lesson instruction. Many teachers choose the whole-class approach in which each new textfilm is presented to the entire class at the same time. In this case, the projection screen should be placed in front of the classroom. If, however, you prefer to separate your class into ability groups, place the projection screen behind a piano or at an angle so that only one section of the class may see it. With small groups, darkening of the room is unnecessary. In many individualized classrooms, filmstrips can be used by children alone or in pairs for review and reinforcement.

Class Organization

Many factors will affect your decisions as to class organization. Local administrative practices and policies may be one factor; the abilities and competencies of the pupils is another; and whether or not homogeneous grouping is used is still another. Whole-class, small groups, partner, and individualized learning patterns all have many advocates. BASIC READING has been designed to work equally well with any method of organization. Some teachers choose to begin the year with whole-group instruction, changing to small-group and individualized instruction as the year progresses and as pupil abilities are identified.

Writing from Dictation

To express ideas creatively in writing, each child must develop a personal skill in the translation of "sounds" into letters, words, and sentences. It is, therefore, recommended that writing from dictation be introduced as soon as correct letter formation has been taught. This activity begins very simply: the teacher pronounces a sound that has already been presented (phoneme), the child listens to that sound, and writes the letter that spells it (grapheme).

Frequent encoding activities, putting into writing what is spoken, provide important opportunities for perfecting each child's writing skills. As soon as the child can write the letters that represent initial, medial, or ending sounds dictated by the teacher, the child can begin to write words from dictation. The teacher can then dictate simple, short phrases and sentences. The teacher should also provide a model from which the child can evaluate and immediately correct what s/he has written.

Writing from dictation begins with correct letter formation and expands to include marker writing, punctuation, and spelling . . . all of which contribute to legible writing. The skill gained as a result of this discipline will enable children to express confidently their creative writing talents.

Communication and Creative Writing

One of the great improvements in the schools of our time springs from the discovery that children thrive on self-expression. A generation or so ago we saw the concept of self-expression as almost a cure-all that would make a child blossom, according to his own "needs" and nature, from encouragement and opportunity rather than direction and discipline. Every child was assumed to have an inherent growth pattern, along with an inherent capacity, that should not be tampered with or disturbed by imposed rigidities of program or instruction.

We have seen these views greatly modified during the past couple of decades, for we have discovered that an excess of permissiveness may be a damaging factor in a child's development. A later understanding finds that children need order, because order produces security, and nothing is more important for the child than security.

With these reservations, we wish, nevertheless, to urge that activities in creative writing that accompany this program be as free as possible. We believe that the children should from their first days in school be encouraged to express themselves by telling recent experiences, making up imaginative stories, and even composing rhymes. A feeling for language develops with its use. In a *setting* of order, restraint, and composure, the child may develop a feeling for communication, a feeling that he is expressing himself to a listening group.

Creative writing should follow the same patterns. That is, the occasion should be one of order and composure, but the writing itself should be free and uninhibited. We should not place undue emphasis upon handwriting or spelling, particularly the latter. Although Basic Reading begins with regular easy spellings, it is no secret that some of the commonest English words are irregularly spelled. If the child is to write freely, he must use these words that he does not know how to spell. It is best to let him spell them according to what letter knowledge he has at the moment, with the understanding that he will learn somewhat later how to spell them correctly. If the creative use of the language is praised, and the question of spelling subordinated as being a practical consideration that will be met later, the child will not be inhibited in trying to write a word that he has not learned how to spell.

The teacher may reward such free writing by reading or having good stories read aloud to the class. Occasionally a good group of stories may be corrected by the teacher and returned for the pupils to take home. It is also stimulating if some of the best stories are correctly typed or printed and posted on the bulletin board, or assembled in a class book. We do not recommend that the primative, uncorrected papers be put on display for the other children to read. The more often a child is asked to correct and rewrite at this level, the shorter and more stilted his future stories will become. Display only the stories that are correct at first writing. If the teacher is affirmative and enthusiastic, the pupils will desire to write, and this is what is wanted most of all.

Regional Pronunciations

American English displays a very wide range of regional pronunciations—so wide that a Maine farmer and a Texas rancher may have some difficulty understanding each other, and perhaps even greater difficulty understanding speakers from certain areas of the Deep South. Yet, as we have said earlier in this Message, these people read the same writing with equal ease. What this proves is that our alphabetic system of writing is an economical *approximation* of the sounds that it records. Wherever you teach, your pupils are going to speak in their local pronunciation and, generally, read in it. The question of refining students' speech toward a more "standard" English than they normally speak is not, strictly, a problem of reading instruction. Where localized pronunciations deviate from the examples in the textbooks, it is advisable to discuss briefly deviations in regional pronunciations while reassuring the pupils that their localized speech patterns are acceptable.

The Use of the Teacher's Editions

The Teacher's Editions for BASIC READING have been designed to present concisely complete suggestions for the development of effective teaching lessons. The suggestions provided are usually more than the teacher has time to use. Therefore, they should not be viewed as mandatory or prescriptive. Instead, the teacher, with intimate knowledge of the abilities of her class, will be able to draw from the suggestions those materials most suitable for her class or teaching group. The suggestions for enrichment, for additional stories and poems, films and filmstrips, and songs may all be used to help to provide for the individual differences in each class.

The suggested materials for the teacher are, for the most part, organized within a logical framework to provide for easy lesson planning. Following the description of the lesson or story with pages involved in the primary program, a section entitled Building Linguistic Skills or Introduction appears. In this section the phoneme-grapheme relationships are presented with pertinent teaching suggestions. Subsequently, sections on Procedure, Guiding Reading for Comprehension, Suggestions for Further Activities, and Enrichment occur. For teacher reference, marginal annotations in a second color highlight skills and objectives.

Materials in the Teacher's Editions are carefully balanced to provide for full utilization of multisensory approaches to learning. Exercises involving auditory discrimination are balanced with exercises involving visual discrimination so that close associations may be made. In addition, there appear exercises utilizing kinesthetic activities for further reinforcement. Suggestions for motivation, vocabulary building, word analysis, creative writing, correlations of auxiliary materials, guidance of silent and oral reading are readily and appropriately placed.

The Teacher's Editions for *Books F, G,* and *H,* contain a Linguistic Elements Guide which may be used effectively with those students who are in need of special help on certain linguistic elements. The teacher may find it helpful to use this Guide in remediation work with students who are, through absence, transfer, or otherwise, in need of special assistance. (*Note:* Permission to reproduce the Linguistic Elements Guide for classroom use is granted by the publisher.)

The Primary Program (Grades One, Two, and Three)

The First-Grade Program

The Grade One program of BASIC READING consists of four books, *A, B, C,* and *D.* These correspond in reading levels to Pre-Primer, Primer, Reader 1-1, and Reader 1-2 respectively. At the back of each reader is a Phoneme-Grapheme Sequence Chart that illustrates the systematic and comprehensive manner in which major English sound-spellings are presented in Grade One.

In the Grade One books, each lesson presents a new linguistic element followed by stories or poems that emphasize it. Rigid control of both the vocabulary and the introduction of these linguistic elements allows the pupil to attack new words and story material successfully. Except for a few "special words," he is never asked to attack words that contain linguistic elements that he has not been taught.

The pupil progresses through the series from the most regular, useful sound-spellings to the less-frequently used and irregular sound-spellings. He also meets other elements such as punctuation marks, run-on sentences, dialogue, paragraphing, and story titles. A full explanation is provided for the teacher at the time the pupil is to be introduced to each new element in the text.

The Second-Grade Program

Book E reviews the phoneme-grapheme presentation of Grade One (*Books A-D*). But instead of more than one hundred elements, taught in more than ninety lessons and stories, *Book E* presents the same linguistic materials condensed into twelve linguistic units. If a class has made good progress through the phonetic system in books *A-D*, the pupils can go through *Book E* rapidly. But, when review or reteaching of linguistics is needed, *Book E* provides the teacher with a full explanation of each sound-spelling and guidance in how to teach it.

The stories and poems in *Book F* are grouped into six sections which reflect a certain unity of tone, style, or subject. The Teacher's Edition suggests a considerable variety of activities and projects that can make use of these groupings; but no teacher need be limited by them.

The Third-Grade Program

The Third-Grade reading program for the pupils consists of two books, *G* and *H*. The pupil is exposed to a wide variety of story content as well as writing styles. Stories and poems include biographies of famous Americans; tales of people of other countries; fairy tales, legends, and myths; stories of American Indians, animals, and contemporary children; and selections from some of the most famous children's fiction.

Glossaries are provided to assist the pupils with the meaning of words encountered in the stories.

In the Teacher's Edition of *Book G* are five special linguistic review units. One linguistic review unit precedes each unit of the reading material. By the end of the fifth unit, the teacher will have reviewed with the pupils all twelve linguistic units previously presented in *Book E*.

BOOK B

Page 1 — Introduction of ar

Building Linguistic Skills

phoneme-grapheme relationships

The combination of **a** and **r** and the resulting new vocabulary. Recognition of the word **are.**

Introduction

Show the children several mounted pictures with the names clearly printed below the picture, such as *car, scarf, park, farm, barn, cart, garden, market, farmer.* Four or five of these pictures placed where the children can see them are sufficient.

introducing the **ar** phoneme

Note: This is the first combination of a vowel with **r.** The sound of **a** is slightly altered. The same **a** sound appears in **father.** The slightly altered **a** is not what is commonly known as a "modified vowel." This term properly applies to the vowels in **her, word, bird, fur,** and **cedar.**

Procedure

Help the children identify the pictures, having them say the words after you. Ask, "What sound did you hear in every word?" After the correct response has been given, have the children look at each word. "What do you see that is the same in each word?" (*ar*) Explain that the letters **ar** spell the /ar/ sound that the children hear. Have several children frame the letters with their hands. List on the board the words from the book, and have the children read the words and draw a line around the **ar** sounds. Put **are** in sentences:

recognizing the grapheme for the **ar** phoneme

> Tag and Rags *are* pets.
> Ned and Tom *are* fat.

Discuss **are,** explaining that the **e** is silent. This is a slightly irregular spelling because the silent **e** does not change the vowel sound. The children will read the word **are** in context.

introducing the word *are*

Use of Text

1. Direct the children to look at their new books; discuss the cover, the title, and the table of contents. Give the children several minutes to look through the book, glancing at the pictures, etc., before having them turn to page 1.

reviewing the care of books

2. Have the children look at the illustration, having them recall the **ar** sound. Use **cart** as a reference if they have difficulty. Ask

what other objects they see in the picture that have this sound. (*star, arms, scarf*)

3. Give the children several seconds to look over the **words** under the picture. Call on individuals to read each word.

checking vocabulary comprehension

4. Review the words by having the children find as fast as possible: (1) a place where animals live (*farm*); (2) something to wear (*scarf*); (3) something you send on someone's birthday (*card*); (4) a part of your body (*arm*), etc.

5. Dictate the word **part.** Have one child write this on the board; a second, change it to **smart;** a third, change **smart** to **dart;** next, change **dart** to **mart,** and so on, using **mar, car, card, cart,** and **art.**

Suggestions for Further Activities

1. Have the children build a list of words using the **ar** sound, such as:

reinforcing the **ar** phoneme through vocabulary development

> part
> dart
> mart
> smart

If you have letter boxes, they can be used here to build words; otherwise the children can print them. If this exercise is used, be sure the board is erased after the class lesson.

providing exercises for independent work

2. Have the children illustrate eight words out of a list of twelve, choosing the ones they wish to use and writing the word beneath each picture.

3. Give the children a duplicated sheet of sentences where **are** appears many times. Have the children underline or draw a line around the word. Put **are** on the board or expose the flash card for those who need to refer to it.

Duplicating Master No. 1 gives practice in recognition of **are.**

Workbook page 1 may also follow this lesson.

Page 2 — The Cats and the Cart

puts

Introduction

presenting a story using the **ar** phoneme

Have the children look at the picture. Help them to identify Tom as a farm worker. Explain that sometimes farm workers are called farm **hands.** Give the children an opportunity to read silently the sign on the cart, and then call on a child to read it to the group. Ask the children what Tom is doing. (*putting more eggs in the cart*)

2

Procedure for Special Word

Hold an object in your hand, such as a crayon. Put it in your pocket or in the crayon box while the children watch you. Elicit the word **put** by asking the children what you did with the crayon. Have the children carry out a few commands that you give them, such as "Put your hand up. Put your right finger on your nose." Then use **puts** in a sentence, such as "Jane puts up her hair every night."

Write **put** on the chalkboard. Explain that, in this word, the **u** does not spell the sound of **u** in **umbrella**. It spells /ù/ as in **cook**. Ask the children to watch your mouth and to listen carefully as you say /ù/. Ask the pupils to make the sound with you. Say **put** several times.

Ask a child what needs to be added to **put** to spell **puts**. Ask him to add it to the word on the chalkboard.

Guiding Reading for Comprehension

Discuss the title of the story with the children. Have the children read the first line to themselves to answer the question, "What kind of worker is Tom?" (*farm hand*) After a child has answered the question, have another child read the line smoothly. Tell the children to look at the second line and then have them read to find out what kind of cart the farm hand has. (*farm cart*) Follow the same procedure as before, getting an answer to the direct question first and then having the sentence read.

Continue to the third sentence and say, "What is on the cart? Put your finger on the word that tells what is on the cart." (*card*) Check the responses and have the sentence read orally. In the last sentence, direct the children to put their fingers under the word that tells what Tom is putting in the cart. (*eggs*) (The children could answer by looking at the pictures. Having them locate and point to the word avoids this.) After all four lines have been studied, have a child read the entire page for continuity before going on to page 3.

Page 3 — The Cats and the Cart
(*continued*)

to

Guiding Reading for Comprehension

Write a few phrases on the chalkboard that include the word **to**. Those in the story can be decoded by the children after a brief presentation of this special word. Explain that the **o** in this word is not short **o** as in **octopus**. It spells long **oo** as in **choo-choo**, and **moo**. Ask the pupils to say these words with you several times, then draw your hand under the word **to** in the first phrase as everyone says the special word with you. Have the pupils read the phrases aloud as a group. Ask for volunteers to use each phrase in a sentence.

Write the word **top** on the chalkboard. Have the pupils say the word. Remove the **p** and ask them to say that word.

building
motivation
through
suspense

Discuss the picture briefly to bring out the suspense of what might be going to happen. Give the children an opportunity to tell what they think might be the end of the story.

Ask the children to read the first sentence to find out where Tom is going. (*off to get a tart*) Discuss what a tart is and where Tom is going to buy it. Have the sentence read smoothly. Ask the children to read the second sentence to find out why Tom didn't notice the cats. (*Tom is far from the cart.*) Ask a child to read the first two sentences aloud. Have the children read the last sentence, then point to the word that tells what animals are at the cart. (*cats*)

Ask the pupils to look at the entire page and frame:

| from the cart | Tom runs |
| to get a tart | Tom is far |

After this opportunity for the children to become familiar with the words, call on a child to read the entire page. Work for fluency and continuity.

Page 4 — The Cats and the Cart
(*conclusion*)

Guiding Reading for Comprehension

enjoying
the humor
of the story

On page 4, let the children enjoy the humor of the story as shown by the picture. Call attention to the question and the question mark. Let the children read silently before calling on a child to read the question. Direct them to the answer in the second sentence and the climax in the final sentence. After having each sentence read aloud, have the entire page read for continuity.

It is suggested that the entire story be read aloud for enjoyment.

Suggestions for Further Activities

nonsense
jingles

Put nonsense jingles on the board to be illustrated. The children may do all, or may choose one and do a larger illustration. Either the teacher or a child may print the jingles for a display.

| A cat in a cart | A part of a tart |
| Is not smart. | Is in the cart. |

| The fast red car | Pat hit his arm. |
| Runs far to a star. | It did no harm. |

dictation

Dictate the story title as well as a few sentences for the children to write, such as:

1. Tom has a tart.
2. Tom runs to the cart.
3. Cats can harm eggs.

Duplicating Master No. 2 can be used here.
Workbook pages 2 and 3 follow this lesson.
S*U*P*E*R Book No. 26, *The Stars*, can be used here.

Enrichment

Aesop, "Belling the Cat," in *Arbuthnot Anthology of Children's Literature,* Scott, Foresman.
Flack, Marjorie, *Angus and the Cat,* Doubleday.
Gag, Wanda, *Millions of Cats,* Coward-McCann.
Jackson, Kathryn and Byron, *Big Farmer Big and Little Farmer Little,* Simon.

Pages 5, 6, 7, and 8 — Two-syllable words

Introduction

her

Play a listening game, having the children clap once as you say, **fast**; then clap twice as you say, **fast er**; continue with **farm, farmer, start, started,** and **dent, dented**. Pronounce these words carefully so that the children will hear both syllables, but pronounce them without distorting the words.

auditory discrimination of two syllables

Procedure—Auditory Activities

As the children clap, explain that each syllable has a sound by itself, almost like a word, as it sometimes is. Continue having the children clap, but have them determine whether they hear a one-syllable or two-syllable word as you read the list:

darted	hunter	under	truck
dump	hunted	into	handed
mend	dart	hand	camper

Visual Activities

Direct the children to open their books to page 5 and notice the illustration of the farmer. Put the word **farmer** on the board. Have the children pronounce it and discover whether the word has one or two syllables. Put a *2* after the word. Return to the picture and ask what the farmer will do. (*farm*) Put this word on the board after the children have clapped their hands to determine the number of syllables. Place a *1* after the word. Ask the children to underline the vowels in **farmer**. (*They find 2.*) Then ask them to

visual discrimination of two syllables

5

underline the vowels in **farm**. (*They find 1*.) Explain that every syllable must have a vowel. It can have more than one, but it must have at least one. When the vowels that we hear are separated by consonants, we have a two-syllable word.

Return to the text and have the children read the words with the **er** ending. After you have presented **farmer**, the children should not have much difficulty with the **er** sound. If they do, put several of the words on the board and move your hand across under the words as you pronounce **faster, starter, tender, hunter**. Put some of these words in simple sentences on the board so that the phoneme-grapheme pattern taught is applied immediately to oral reading. For example:

> Tom ran faster and faster.
> The farmer fed the pigs.

Have the children find the two-syllable words and underline them. Also have them draw a line around the two vowels in each.

Procedure for Special Word

presenting the special word *her*

After reading the **er** two-syllable words, call attention to the word **her**. Try to get a child's response. It may be necessary to have him cover **h**, discover **er**, and add **h**. Before leaving this word, ask how many syllables there are in it. The word **her** is special because it has only one syllable in a group of two-syllable words. It is not an irregular word.

Note: It may be desirable to end the lesson here and spend time in reviewing the words presented.

Procedure for Page 6

Follow the same procedure with the **ed** words on page 6. Before reading the two-syllable words which are not formed by a suffix, explain that all two-syllable words are not formed by adding an ending to a whole word. Some words start as two syllables. Progress slowly, helping the children to see two syllables before reading a word aloud. Avoid having the children pronounce one syllable before they are ready to read the entire word.

introducing the suffix *ed* pronounced as a syllable

Use these two-syllable words in simple sentences on the board so that the phoneme-grapheme patterns taught are applied immediately to oral reading. For example:

> Ted started the car.
> Ann mended her rug.
> Ted has a garden.

Have the children find the two-syllable words and underline them. Also, have them draw a line around the two vowels.

Note: The words in the green box are all useful, two-syllable words.

Except for **into,** all have two short vowel sounds. Since **to** was taught as a special word on page 3, the word **into** should present no difficulty here.

Page 4 of the accompanying workbook may be used following this lesson.

Procedure for Pages 7 and 8

In introducing the words on pages 7 and 8, tell the children that some words that end in **ed** do not have two syllables. The ending of these words is /d/ or /t/ instead of /ed/. Do not dwell on these differences as the pronunciations will seem quite natural to the children. They will meet these endings again in *Book C,* pages 44 through 47.

introducing the alternate pronunciation of the ed syllable

Suggestions for Further Activities

1. Put two-syllable words on a ditto sheet; have the children find and circle the vowels. Be sure the words you select for duplication do not contain vowel digraphs.

2. On a ditto sheet, list at random short-vowel words of one syllable and two syllables. Have the children put a *1* or a *2* in front of each word, depending on the number of syllables they see and hear.

reinforcing syllable discrimination

> *Example:*   *2* tender
>   *1* mark
>   *2* harder

Duplicating Master No. 3 is similar to the above.
Workbook page 5 may follow this lesson.
S*U*P*E*R Books No. 27 and 28 can be used here.

Enrichment

Some simple nursery rhymes, like "Little Miss Muffet," "Little Jack Horner," "Lucy Locket," and "Little Tommy Tucker," may be said in unison, with the children clapping rhythmically. The titles may be repeated slowly so that the children recognize two-syllable words.

clapping nursery rhymes

Page 9 — Words beginning with / w /

were

Building Linguistic Skills

Play a game to introduce /w/ as an initial sound. Tell the children you are thinking of a word that begins like **wiggle.** Give them a clue, such as, "It makes the leaves dance." (*wind*) Tell the children you are thinking of another word that begins like **wiggle** and **wind;**

introduction of the initial w phoneme

it is what you need to drink every day. (*water*) Pause in the game and see who can repeat all three words that begin with /w/. Continue giving clues to words with **w** in the initial position.

Ask a child to find and name the letter **w** in the alphabet. Ask the children to note whether this letter is near the beginning or the end of the alphabet. If there are children in the group whose names begin with **w,** write their names on the chalkboard.

Procedure

providing
auditory
discrimination
activities

1. Say the following words, and have the children repeat them after you:

want	won't	wake	wet
will	water	wear	wait
weather	way	wind	witch

2. Ask the children to listen carefully to three words you are going to say. Explain that two words will begin with /w/ and one will not. Let the children repeat the two words they hear that begin with /w/. If the children need the practice, have them say each word group after you, then say only the two words that have /w/ in the initial position. Listed below are some word groups you could use:

wag	west	we	wear	wig
will	sun	weak	gown	pig
yell	wind	bend	warm	went

3. Have the children turn to page 9. See if they can find the letter **W** in the art. Ask questions about the art that will elicit the words **wagon, water,** and **wet.** Ask what letter represents the beginning sound in those words (*w*).

pronouncing
words in the
yellow and
green blocks

Ask the children to look at all the words in the yellow block, and to point to the words **wet** and **wagon.** Ask them to read the rest of the words in the yellow block, and to use them in sentences. Ask if there is any word that does not begin with **w.**

Help the children with the pronunciation of the words in the green block. Here **a** does not spell the short vowel sound as in **astronaut.** The vowel sound is somewhat modified or changed. In these words, the **a** is pronounced more like the short **o** in **octopus.** Have the children look carefully at each word in the green block as you say them, then ask the children to pronounce each word after you.

4. Here are some simple riddles to use, if desired. Read them to the children and let them guess the answers (words that begin with /w/).

building
vocabulary
through
riddles

I help to fly kites.	I am a toy.
I make sailboats go.	Children ride in me.
I move the clouds.	I can be used to haul things.
I am the (wind).	I am a (wagon).

In some places it snows.
I am the opposite of summer.
At the North Pole I last a
    long, long time.
I am (winter).

I am something wet.
Children like to play in me.
I help plants and trees to grow.
Fish swim in me.
I am (water).

5. Have the children read the words on page 9 to locate the four two-syllable words. Remind them to look for words with two vowels. Develop **western** from **west**. Ask the pupils where the **er** sound is in this word. Help them to pronounce the word as a whole, rather than sound it out painfully in parts. Have the children say the two-syllable words aloud. Say all the words and have the children raise one hand when you pronounce a one-syllable word and both hands when they hear a two-syllable word.

6. Put some of the words from page 9 into sentences. Ask the pupils how many words they hear in each sentence that begin with /w/. Dictate some of the sentences for the pupils to write.

writing from dictation

1. The wagon went faster and faster.
2. The wagon went into the water.
3. The west wind is soft.
4. Were his arms wet?
5. Nan went to a farm in the west.
6. Did Ann win a wig?

Put **er** on the chalkboard. Ask a pupil to say the sound these letters represent when they are written together /er/. Print **her** below **er**. Ask the pupils to read **er**, and **her**, then add **were**. Help the pupils see that **were** is pronounced as if it were spelled **wer**. Cover the final **e** and have them say the word. The final **e** spells no sound in this special word.

presenting the special word *were*

Suggestions for Further Activities

1. Some of these words have a variety of meanings; this is, therefore, an excellent time to have children illustrate words beginning with **w**. These do not have to be words the children can read, as long as they can tell you what the words represent, such as: **wave, wind** (long or short **i**), **wet, water, west, wig, wag, win.** There are many possibilities for vocabulary enrichment here, and this should never be overlooked. Assign four pictures of anything they can think of that begins with **w**.

illustrating words that begin with **w**

2. Have the children find four magazine pictures of objects whose names begin with **w**.

3. Put the following sentences on the board to be illustrated:

1. Ted's arms are wet.
2. Ed has a red wagon.
3. The pig is in a wig.
4. The car went fast.

Workbook page 6 follows this lesson.

9

Enrichment

Read any stories or poems about the wind—for example:
"Who Has Seen the Wind," by Christina Rosetti, in *Time for Poetry*, Scott, Foresman.
"Wind on the Hill," by A. A. Milne, in *Now We Are Six*, Dutton.
"The Wind and the Sun," *Aesop's Fables*, Lippincott.

Page 10 — Wags Gets Wet

Introduction

Begin by discussing the title of the story and the pictures on pages 10 and 11. Ask where the family is and what is happening. Encourage the children to use their imaginations to speculate about how the dog got in this predicament and about what might be going to happen to him. After several ideas have been shared, suggest that the children read the story to find out what really happened.

Guiding Reading for Comprehension

Tell the children to read the first two sentences silently. Then ask them to frame the name of the dog (*Wags*) and the color of the wagon. (*red*) Have these two sentences read aloud.

Ask the children to read the next two sentences silently to find out how the wagon went. (*faster and faster*) Ask what word could be used instead of **run** in the third sentence. (*go*)

Have the third and fourth sentences read aloud. Explain that the expression used and the pace of the reading can create a mental picture of the wagon going faster and faster. Demonstrate by reading the two sentences yourself. Call on a few children to read the sentences aloud. Let the others comment on whether or not the reader gave the feeling that the wagon was out of control and going faster and faster. Discuss how the little girl must feel and how the dog feels.

Page 11 — Wags Gets Wet
(continued)

Guiding Reading for Comprehension

Ask the children to read the first two sentences (lines) to learn the names of the others in the picture. (*Pam* and *Topper*) Ask someone to demonstrate what **darted** means. What other word could the author have used? (*ran*) Have the children close their eyes as you read the sentence to them, first with the word **ran,** then with the word **darted.** Ask them which makes them see a more exciting picture in their minds.

Ask who is out in front (*Wags*), Who is behind him? (*Pam*) Who is behind her? (*Topper*)

Continue to guide their comprehension skills with questions after silent reading. Questions you might use are:

Why was Pam running so fast?

Why was she anxious to stop the wagon?

Ask what other word could be used instead of **harmed.** (*hurt*) Have four children share in reading the story aloud from the beginning to the bottom of page 11. Excitement should build as each pair of lines is read.

reading to
answer
questions

Page 12 — Wags Gets Wet
(*continued*)

Ask the children to examine the picture and to describe what happened. Ask them to think of words that would tell how Pam felt. (Try to avoid the "happy—sad" limitations. Encourage such words as *worried, afraid, anxious, excited.*)

recognizing
emotions

Have the children read the first sentence silently and frame the word that tells what the wagon did (*stopped*). What did Wags do? (*He didn't stop but was tossed into the water.*)

After silent reading, call attention to the exclamation point at the end of the third sentence. Explain that it is used here to show excitement. Demonstrate by reading without, then with, excitement.

explaining the
exclamation
point

Have the children read silently to learn what Pam did. Have the page read aloud for fluency and continuity.

Page 13 — Wags Gets Wet
(*conclusion*)

Allow time for the children to enjoy the illustration. Ask how they think Pam feels now. What clues are there in the picture? How does Wags feel? Ask them what they think Wags is about to do (*lick Pam's face*). Discuss whether or not it was dangerous for Pam to dart in after Wags. What will Pam do next?

discussing
the picture

Give the children every opportunity to think creatively and to express their ideas.

Guiding Reading for Comprehension

Have the children read the first two sentences silently. After they have read the third sentence, ask them what stopped the wagon from going into the pond. (*a log*) Was the wagon harmed? (*yes*)

11

How? (*It was dented.*) Discuss what **dented** means, or show the pupils what happens when a can is hit with a hammer. Have children read the entire page aloud; then if appropriate for your group, have them read the entire story aloud for continuity. Emphasize reading with expression.

Allow time for the children to discuss any similar experience that this story may bring to mind. If they need to be prompted or stimulated, ask: Have you ever gotten your clothes wet when in wading? When running in a sprinkler, a fire hydrant, or the ocean? How did it feel?

relating
personal
experiences
to the story

Suggestions for Further Activities

1. Put the following sentences on the chalkboard. Ask the children to read them silently, then to choose a word from the list to complete each sentence. After sufficient time, call upon a child to read the first sentence aloud, completing it with the word he thinks fits best. Let him choose someone to draw a line through the correct word he has chosen from the list, or have him write the number of the sentence in front of it. Continue in this manner until all the sentences have been read aloud.

Ask the entire group to read the sentences aloud together, supplying the correct words from the list.

1. Wags got into the (*wagon*).	darted
2. The wagon started to go (*faster*).	pond
3. Pam (*darted*) after it.	wagon
4. (*Topper*) ran after Pam.	faster
5. Into the (*pond*) went Wags.	forest
6. The red wagon was (*dented*).	Topper
	dented
	garden
	Tom

providing an
exercise for
independent
study

2. A similar exercise can be duplicated for independent work with the children writing in the correct word to complete each sentence.

3. Duplicating Master No. 4 can be used here.

Enrichment

Use any stories you like about wagons. For example:

Allen, Marie Louise, "Jim and Scotch and the Little Red Wagon," in *Tales Told Under the Blue Umbrella*, The Macmillan Company.

Baruch, Dorothy, "The Express Wagon," in *Tales Told Under the Blue Umbrella*, The Macmillan Company.

Cording, Ruth, "Luke and His Little Red Wagon," in *Read Me More Stories*, Thomas Y. Crowell Company.

Page 14 — Words with /war/

Building Linguistic Skills

wa modified by r.

Introduction

Show the children a picture of a frog with a wart, or use the picture on this page of the man getting warm.

introducing the
war pattern

Procedure

Have the children find the word **warm** under the picture. Call on the children to read the word **warm**. Call the children's attention to the spelling. The children will hear the new sound of **a.** Explain that many times, the **ar** sounds almost like **or.** Put the words on the board from page 14. Have the children read each one as you put it on. Develop **wart, warm,** and **swarm** from **war.** Do not neglect the meanings of these words. Use **war** words in simple phrases or sentences:

war in the west
a warm wind
Warren is wet.
Ned was warm.

A swarm of wasps
Water is warm.
Was the water warm?
The frog has a wart.

Have the children take turns reading the phrases and sentences; then pronounce a single word and have a child frame it and pronounce it. If you think it is needed for fluency, have the child, or another child, read the entire phrase containing the word.

Incidentally, in oral reading, bring out the common pronunciation of **was.** Run your hand across from left to right to prevent confusion of **was** and **saw.**

preventing
confusion of
was and saw

Suggestions for Further Activities

1. If some of the suggestions on page 9 were not done at this time, they could be used here.
2. Simple phrases or sentences can be copied and illustrated:

providing
independent
exercises

a red wagon	a warm hat
in the water	Wags is a dog.

Introduction

interpreting emotions of story characters

Discuss the picture, having the children see the happy expression on Rags' face and the mixed emotions which Ted is experiencing. Discuss why Ted feels as he does, etc.

Guiding Reading for Comprehension

finding the title

Have the children read silently to find out whom the story is about. (*Ted and Rags*) Ask, "What is the title?" (*Ted and Rags*) "Who can find a word beginning with *w*?" (*water*) Have the children locate and read these words. Ask, "How does the water feel?" (*warm*) "What did Ted want to do?" (*run in the water*) "What did he *not* want to do?" (*get wet*) "What happened to Rags?" (*got wetter and wetter*) After these questions for silent reading have been asked, have several children read the page aloud. Divide the text into three parts and have individual children read each part; then have one child read the entire page for continuity.

oral reading for continuity

said

Introduction

relating personal experiences

In the discussion of the picture, give one or two children an opportunity to relate similar personal experiences.

Guiding Reading for Comprehension

developing punctuation skills: quotation marks

Explain that quotation marks show the exact words someone has said. Ask, "What did Ted say to Rags?" (*Get it, Rags, get it*) Have the children read the words between the quotation marks first silently, then orally, emphasizing expression. Say, "Read the way you would say it if Rags were your dog." Ask the children who they think said these words. As they respond (*Ted*), explain that this is just what the story says. Read the first sentence for them.

oral reading with expression

Continue to develop expressive reading by asking the children to study the second sentence and read it the way they think Ted said it. Let several children read it the way they would say it.

Finish the page by having the children read silently to find out what happened to Rags. (*got wetter and wetter*) Call on individuals to read each sentence. One of the better readers can probably be allowed to read the entire page.

Before going on, ask the children what the special word is at the bottom of the page. (*said*)

14

Pages 17 and 18 — Ted and Rags
(*continued*)

Introduction

for

Discuss whether Rags got the gun. Recall that Ted did not want to get wet. Then have the children turn to page 18 and enjoy the humor in the situation. Be sure the children understand what the art is illustrating.

Put **far** on the chalkboard or on a flashcard, and ask the children to read it aloud. Write or flash **for,** and ask the children to decode the new word the best they can. The **o** is modified or changed by the **r,** so the children will need some assistance to pronounce it correctly. Have them say **far** and **for** several times after you. Cover the **f** in **for,** and see if the children recognize the word **or.**

introducing the special word *for*

Have the children look at the special word in the red box at the bottom of page 17. Ask several children to give sentences using this word. If appropriate, help the children become aware that **for** and **four** sound alike but that /or/ is spelled two different ways.

Guiding Reading for Comprehension

Have the children read the first two sentences. Ask who got the gun (*Rags*) and where Ted went. (*to Rags*) In presenting the next sentences, ask what Rags did. (*got the water off*)

On page 18 ask where the water went. (*from Rags to Ted*) Have the children look for quotation marks. Ask who said the words. (*Ted*) Review the special word *said*. In the last sentences, ask what Ted said about the water and how it felt. (*wet and warm*)

reviewing quotation marks

Follow the same plan for oral reading. These two pages may be too long for some children to read. The story is a good one to re-read to develop oral expression.

Discuss the humor of the story and the children's personal experiences. It is better to allow free discussion before or after the story rather than risk breaking up the continuity in the middle.

Other activities may include illustrations of the children's own stories. They may dictate short experiences with their pets, funny things that have happened, or any similar stories, that the teacher can print under each child's picture.

developing creative writing

Procedure for Special Word

This exercise to reinforce the word **said** may be introduced following the oral reading, or it may be a separate lesson.

Put **said Ted** on the board. Under it, put **Ted said,** and have a child read each one. Add **Pam said,** or use names of the children in

reinforcing the special word *said*

15

the group, writing the word **said** several times. Have the group read these phrases before returning to the book, page 16.

Have a child read the entire first sentence. Have the children study the second sentence and then read it with much expression.

Suggestions for Further Activities

exercises for independent work

1. Copy the following sentences on the chalkboard, and have the children complete them as a group, or duplicate them so that each child may have his own. The children are to write **said** in each sentence.

    1. Tom _____, "Run, Nan, run fast."
    2. "Nan can run fast," _____ Ned.
    3. "Run, Ann," _____ Ed. "Run faster."
    4. "Ann did win," Tom _____.

Be sure to have the children read the sentences orally, either before or after they have written the word in each blank.

phrases for dictation

2. Dictate phrases for the children to write, such as the following:

for him	for her	for Mom
for his dad	for **Pam**	for *(child's name)*

3. Provide opportunities for the children to practice writing letters of the alphabet. In some cases, suggest they illustrate them by adding a picture of something that either begins or ends with that letter. Regular lined writing paper should be provided if the children are to copy from the board, write from dictation, or practice forming letters.

Duplicating Master No. 5 may be used here.

Page 19 — aw as in saw

Building Linguistic Skills

Short **a** modified by **w**.

Introduction

introducing the word *saw* and the **aw** pattern

A picture can be used here to illustrate a dog's paw, a fawn, or any of the words listed. If these pictures are difficult to find, use three or four mounted pictures of objects. Flash very quickly; then say, "What did you see?" The child will answer, "I saw a cat," or "I saw a _____" (whatever he could see in the rapid exposure). Print his response on the board: "Ned saw a cat." Expose another picture and repeat the question, and again have the child respond

16

"I saw _____." Again put it on the board: "Jack saw a _____."
After several sentences have been put on the board, have the children find and frame **saw**.

practicing auditory discrimination of the **aw** pattern

If the pictures are used, print under each picture (or over, if picture is on chalkboard) a simple sentence, such as: *The dog's paw is tan.* Give the children time to study the picture and sentence before reading it. Have a child frame **paw**.

Write a few **aw** words on cards or on the chalkboard. Point out that, in these words, **a** spells nearly the same sound as **o** in **octopus**. Have the children say the **aw** words aloud that you put on the board, then turn to page 19. Ask what the man has in his hand and what he is doing with it. (*a saw; sawing*) Have the pupils read all the words aloud. Discuss the double meaning of **saw**. (*as a noun and as a verb*) Ask individuals to use the words in sentences to clarify meanings. Encourage the children to think of multiple meanings of as many of the words as possible.

Dictate a few simple sentences for the children to write using **saw**:

sentences for dictation

1. Ted saw a cat.
2. Pam saw a car.
3. The hunter saw a fawn.
4. The fawn saw the hunter.

Suggestions for Further Activities

Put the following sentences on the board for a written exercise, or duplicate them. Read and fill in the blank in the first sentence with the children.

exercises for independent work

                saw   was
1. Nan _____ a cat.
2. It _____ a pet cat.
3. It _____ in a hat.
4. The cat _____ Nan.
5. Nan _____ it run fast.

Workbook pages 7 and 8 follow this lesson.
Duplicating Master No. 6 can be used here.

★

Page 20 — A Fawn at Dawn

Introduction

Have the children look at the picture on page 20. Ask what animal they see. (*a fawn*) If no one knows, you may tell them. Tell

17

them that a fawn is a baby animal. Ask what animal it will be when it grows up. (*deer*) If time permits, you may discuss names for other baby animals that are different from their adult names. Some examples might be: **lamb—sheep; calf—cow; kitten—cat; puppy—dog; colt—horse.**

Guiding Reading for Comprehension

Have a child read the title. Explain what time of the day it is (*dawn*) Have the pupils read the first sentence silently. Then ask what the boys' names are. (*Sam, Win*) Ask what Sam handed Win. (*a gun*) Have them read the second sentence to find what Win handed Sam. (*a dart*) Have a child read these two sentences. Ask the children why they think Sam and Win have a gun and a dart. Build suspense.

Have the children read the next two sentences. Ask, "Where did Sam and Win go?" (*into the forest*) "What was in the forest?" (*fawns*) Have these sentences read orally. Someone may read the whole page, if you wish.

Page 21 — A Fawn at Dawn (*continued*)

Guiding Reading for Comprehension

Continue with questions to develop page 21 with a procedure similar to the one used for page 20. Ask questions such as, "What did Win see?" (*a fawn*) "What word describes the fawn?" (*fat*) "When did he see it?" (*at dawn*) You may wish to have the children frame the words *fawn* and *dawn* when they answer the questions. "Did the fawn see Sam and Win?" (*yes*) Have the sentences read orally. "What did the fawn do?" (*run*) Have them frame the word that tells how the fawn ran. (*fast*) "Where did it run?" (*into the winter camp tent*)

Page 22 — A Fawn at Dawn (*continued*)

Introduction

Discuss the picture. Ask the children where they think the fawn is. Ask them if they think Sam and Win will find it. Read the page to find out.

Guiding Reading for Comprehension

Have the children read the first sentence silently to find out what Sam and Win did. (*hunted the fawn*) Ask the children to read the next sentence and tell where the fawn was. (*in the tent*) In the third sentence, ask "What did Sam do then?" (*started to the farm*) Ask the children why he is going to the farm. (*couldn't find the fawn*) Have them read the last sentence aloud.

Page 23 — A Fawn at Dawn (*conclusion*)

Guiding Reading for Comprehension

Continue right on to the end of the story by asking questions. Ask, "Where did Win and Sam go?" (*to the farm*) "Why did Win want to go?" (*to get warm*) "What season was it?" (*winter*) Have someone read the third sentence that tells what the winter did to Win. Finally, ask, "Did Win and Sam hurt the fawn?" (*no*) Review the entire story by having it read aloud. Call on several students so that all may participate as often as possible.

Now you may want to help them draw a conclusion. Have the pupils go back to page 22 and read the last sentence. (*Sam must not harm a fawn.*) Then have them read the last sentence on page 23. (*Win and Sam did not harm the fawn.*) Have the children discuss why the boys did not harm the fawn. Was it because they did not want to be cruel? Or did they really love animals? Or was it because they could not catch the fawn and they were getting very cold? Try to have the children bring out these alternatives instead of suggesting them yourself.

A follow-up activity for this story would be a discussion of taking care of animals. The children will be familiar with taking care of pets, but here you may bring out how we take care of animals in the forest. Also discuss how these animals find ways to protect themselves. Bring out the fact that the fawn hid because it was afraid. Animals are often afraid of people; that is why they run from us. Have the children share their personal experiences with animals in the park, camping, etc.

Suggestions for Further Activities

1. Make a duplicated sheet like the one that follows. Have the children underline those sentences that are true. If you prefer, these sentences could be put on the board and the comprehension exercise could be combined with a writing lesson.

19

1. Win handed Sam a gun.
2. Win handed Sam a dart.
3. Sam and Win went into the forest.
4. Cats were in the forest.
5. The fawn ran to the farm.
6. Sam and Win went into the tent.
7. Sam harmed the fawn.
8: It was winter.

using pictures
for a bulletin
board display

providing
enrichment

2. Have the children draw or look for pictures of animals in magazines. Classify these animals as wild animals or pets. This project could make an attractive bulletin board display.

S*U*P*E*R Book No. 29, *Summer and Winter*, follows this lesson.

Enrichment

Salton, Felix, *Bambi.*

Page 24 — Special sound of ow as in cow

phoneme-
grapheme
relationships

Building Linguistic Skills

One sound of **o** when followed by **w.** Phoneme-grapheme pattern as heard in **cow.**

Introduction

introducing
the **ow** pattern

Allow the children to enjoy the humor in the picture and ask what they think this little "engine" is saying. What do they say when they pinch their fingers or stub their toes? (*ow*)

Procedure

practicing
auditory
recognition of
the **ow** pattern

Put **ow** on the board and call on a child to "make it say **how.**" Call on another child to change it (or rewrite it) to **now.** Continue through the five words **how, now, cow, down,** and **town.**

Put on the board for practice in reading aloud fluently:

a tan cow
down town
how fast
down to the farm
starts now
saw a cow

Use Word Recognition cards for rapid drill.
Workbook page 9 may be used here.

Pages 24 and 25 — The Cow and the Frog

Introduction

The illustration for this story is humorous enough to serve as motivation. Discuss the comical situation and ask what the children think will happen next, and why. Ask, "Can the cow swim? Can the frog swim?"

using humor as motivation for reading

Guiding Reading for Comprehension

Have the children read the title silently, and then aloud. This will reinforce the **ow** sound previously learned.

reinforcing the ow pattern

Questions for guided reading: "Where was the frog sitting?" (*on a raft*) (This cannot be guessed from the picture.) "Who saw the frog? (*a tan cow*) What did the cow do?" (*sat down*) (These three sentences may be read aloud as a thought unit at this point if the teacher so desires.) "What happened to the raft? Find the word that tells in which direction it went." (*down*) "Now find the word that tells where the cow is sitting." (*water*)

checking comprehension

Direct the children to read the last sentence so that they can read the entire story smoothly.

Have several children read the story aloud for pleasure as well as for fluency and expression.

Workbook page 10 follows this lesson.

Here is an opportunity to encourage original, imaginative stories. Nonsense stories, rhymes, and jingles can provoke creativity as well as appreciation for this type of literature.

encouraging creativity

Page 26 — Words with l

Building Linguistic Skills

l as an initial consonant, part of a blend, in medial, and in terminal positions.

phoneme-grapheme relationships

Introduction

In learning the nursery rhymes, the children may have recited or sung, "Mary Had a Little Lamb." If so, have them recite it again, showing them a picture of a little lamb from a farm storybook or from your own collection. If they are not familiar with the rhyme, teach or read it now.

Procedure

introducing
the initial
l phoneme

1. Repeat **little lamb,** having the children repeat after you several times.

2. For variety have the children find words in the yellow block that rhyme with the words in the list below. Say, "pot," and have the child respond, "lot." Explain that all the words must begin like **lamb.** Other words to use:

practice in
rhyming words

bad	better	ramp
hog	rip	fist
cap	fast	frost
wet	mess	

3. Have a child point to l in the alphabet. Then dictate some of the three-letter words that begin with l for board work or for written exercises.

recognizing
the l phoneme
in a medial
position

4. Call one child to the board, explain that this is going to be more difficult, and have the entire class watch as you dictate **clap.** (The meaning of **clap** is easier for all children, probably, than **clam** or **clan.**) After all the children have seen the initial blend, continue dictating, using the words from the book. These words should be developed while all the children watch the child at the board so that all of the blends will be seen and heard by everyone.

5. As these words are spelled, make a duplicate list higher on the board or arrange a duplicate list of flash cards in the card holder. Use this as a review, having the children find dictated words after the writing part of the lesson has been completed. (This writing can slow the lesson down and cause it to lag. If this is the case, dictate some words from each blend group, and then develop the remainder of the list without the writing experiences.) Use the words in sentences frequently; for instance—"Find **clam. Clams** live in the sand under the water and they are good to eat. Find **clam.**" "Find **plug.** I will put a **plug** in the sink so the water won't go away. Find **plug.**"

developing
writing skills

Note: In developing the lesson, the teacher should include as many, or as few, of the words from the book as necessary for the particular group.

6. After the words have been reviewed several times visually, remove the list and have the children listen and locate the initial, medial, and terminal sounds. There are a variety of ways that this may be done:

recognizing
initial, medial,
and terminal
sounds

a) Say, "log"; ask, "What is the first sound?
What is the name of the first letter?"
b) Say, "class"; ask, "What is the last sound?"
c) Say, "glad"; ask, "What is the last letter?"
d) Say, "flat"; ask, "What is the vowel sound in the middle?"
e) Say, "slip"; ask, "What is the name of the vowel in the middle?"

Use the terms *sound* and *name of the letter,* as well as *first, last, middle,* and *vowel.*

Suggestions for Further Activities

1. Have the children:
    a) find four things that begin with l in magazines.
    b) draw four things that begin with l.

exercises for independent work

2. Write the following list on the board and have the children complete the words. Be sure that the children understand that these must be real words that they can read. If the children make words which have not been listed, this should, of course, be praised.

gla___   l___st   cl___p   lo___
fl___p   ___ap   pl___g   sla___

Duplicating Master No. 7 can be used here.
Workbook pages 11 and 12 can also follow this lesson.

Enrichment

Poem: de la Mare, Walter, "The Cupboard," in Arbuthnot, *Time for Poetry,* Scott, Foresman.

Nursery Rhyme: "Lucy Locket," in *Anthology of Children's Literature,* Houghton Mifflin.

Story: "The Lion and the Mouse," in *Aesop's Fables,* Lippincott.

providing enrichment activities

Page 27 — Words having double l

Building Linguistic Skills

The double ll at the end of the word and the exceptional phoneme resulting from **ull.**

phoneme-grapheme relationships

Introduction

Have the nursery rhyme "Jack and Jill" printed on a chart so that the children can see it, or have them recite it. If they can see it, have them read it in unison. Have them find, or recall, all the words that end in an l sound. List these words on the board.

teaching a nursery rhyme

Procedure

1. After you have listed *Jill, hill,* and *fell,* ask if someone notices anything unusual. Call attention, if necessary, to the double l.

introducing the ll pattern for the l phoneme

2. Have the children open their books to page 27. Explain that just as the sound of **a** is changed or modified by a **w**, it is also changed when followed by an **l**. Put the word **saw** on the board and have it read. Ask for the sound of **a** in **saw**.

3. Direct the children's attention to the first word on the page. Call on various children to read the words in the yellow box. These words should present no difficulty.

teaching the
irregular **ull**
pattern

4. Treat the irregular words in the green box and the word **put** as follows:

Write the following sentences on the chalkboard:

Put the log down.   Put the flag up.

Have a child read these sentences aloud for the class. If he pronounces the word **put**, pŭt, ask him if the sentence makes sense. Point out that here **u** spells the sound of short **oo** as in **cook**. In the sentences, change **put** to **pull**, and have a child read them to the group. Erase the sentences, and have the child recall **pull**. Write it on the chalkboard. Ask how **pull** can be changed to **full**. Write: *The pan is full,* and have it read aloud. Ask a child to change **full** to **pull** again. Ask for a volunteer to add what is needed to change **pull** to **pullet,** a small hen. Have **put, pull, full,** and **pullet** on flashcards, and review these words for two or three minutes.

Modifications of *a* with *l* and *ll*

introducing the
modified **a** with
l and **ll**

Put on the board: *Tom will pull the small wagon.* Have the children find words with **l**'s and underline them. When someone has underlined **small**, reread it, or have a child read it as you move your hand under the sentence so that everyone will recognize **small**. Ask what the name of the vowel is. It is enough now to recall that other letters (**r** and **w**) changed the sound of **a**, and **l** can change it too. Discuss with the children, the sentences with the modified words on page 27, using the board, and having them find and frame the words as you say them.

Suggestions for Further Activities

providing
exercises for
independent
work

1. Have the children illustrate phrases or sentences using words beginning or ending with **l**, such as:

a lad at the mill
The log will fall.
a plant on the wall
Pull the log up the hill.

2. Use Duplicating Master No. 8 or put simple sketches on a duplicated sheet and supply part of the word. Have the children complete the word. Here is an example:

24

gl_ss   _ill   _ant

h_met   wa_   h_ll

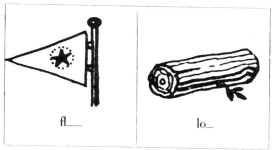

fl_   lo_

Enrichment

Use the poem on page 28 for enrichment.

providing
enrichment

Page 28 — A poem: Ellen on a hill-top

Introduction

This simple lyrical poem creates a picture, not a story.

enjoying
a poem

Procedure

1. Allow the children an opportunity to read the poem silently.
Have them locate all the words having double l's. List these words

locating
the ll pattern

25

on the board and review them so that the poem will present no difficulty when read.

2. Ask what the little girl's name is. Ask where she is. (*Ellen, on a hill-top*)

3. Have the group read the poem in unison.

4. Have several children read it aloud alone.

5. Ask why the word **still** is repeated. If no one can answer, reread it to the group, and as you reread it, have the children clap their hands lightly, feeling the rhythm. They will feel the need for three syllables at the end.

6. Have the entire group read the poem again in unison.

Page 13 of the accompanying workbook may be used following this lesson.

Page 29 — Flat Sam

Introduction

Have the children discuss the picture, identifying the names of the objects, since clams may be unfamiliar to some children. Ask how many clams they see, and have them count them going from left to right.

It may be necessary to explain that clams are a kind of shellfish that lives in the sand, under the water. Explain that people can dig them out of the sand when the tide goes out. They have two shells that are tightly closed but open up when they are cooked. The inside is good to eat.

Guiding Reading for Comprehension

Have the children study and read the title of the story. Tell them that as they read the story, they will find out who "Flat Sam" is.

In the first sentence, have them find the "number" word (*ten*) and the word that tells what kind of clams they were. (*small*) Have them frame the phrase telling where they sat. (*in the sand*) In the second sentence, have them do the same. (*under a log*) For the third sentence, ask how the water felt. (*warm*) Have these three sentences read as a unit. The next sentence tells what clams can do that some other animals cannot do. Have the children find the answer. (*dig in the sand*) Have them read the last sentence aloud.

Pages 30 and 31 — Flat Sam (*continued*)

Guiding Reading for Comprehension

Discuss the picture. Ask, "What is the turtle doing? Why are the clams digging?" Tell the children that the first sentence will tell them what the turtle's name is. Have them find it silently and respond. (*Flat Sam*)

interpreting a picture

The second sentence tells what Flat Sam wanted to do. This is a long sentence, and after a child has answered the question about what Sam wanted to do, have the sentence read aloud. (*to get the clams*) Call the children's attention to the quotation marks in the next part. Review their significance, and then have the class read the first sentence to find out who was talking. (*a clam*) Explain that *ed* added to *call* does not make a second syllable. Direct them to read what the clam said. "What did he tell them to do first?" (*dig*) "Next?" (*get under the sand*) "Where did he tell them to dig?" (*far into the sand*)

reviewing punctuation: quotation marks

The children may be familiar with exclamation marks from other experiences. Help them to pronounce "exclamation." Call attention to the mark, and ask how many exclamation marks the children can find on page 30. Ask them what they think this mark means. Stress that an exclamation mark shows excitement. Have a child read the last three sentences aloud as he thinks the clam would have said them. Ask the listeners if the reader showed excitement as he read.

developing punctuation skills: exclamation point

Now discuss page 31 with the children.

Ask the children how Flat Sam went after the clams. (*swam*) Have them point to the word. Ask them to frame the words in the second sentence that tell what the clams did. (*dug and dug*) Call attention to the next sentence, which is a question. Have it read silently, then aloud, for proper inflection.

reading aloud for proper inflection

In the second group of sentences, ask how Flat Sam swam. (*fast*)

Page 32 — Flat Sam (*conclusion*)

Introduction

Here is the conclusion, as shown in the picture: a happy ending for everyone but Flat Sam.

Guiding Reading for Comprehension

Have the children look at page 32. As the children read the first group of sentences, ask questions similar to those on page 28.

checking comprehension

27

"What noise did the water make?" (*slap, slap*) "Did Flat Sam get the clams?" (*no*) Have the sentence that gives this answer read silently and aloud.

In the last group of sentences ask, "Where were the clams?" (*in the sand*) Direct the children to read both sentences silently; then call on a child to read them aloud.

reading
for fluency
and continuity

You may prefer to have each thought unit read completely before going on to the next group of sentences, or you may follow the pattern of having the entire page studied and then read aloud. It is not necessary, if this last system is used, to have one child read the entire page, but two or three children can read the page without discussion or interruption, for fluency and continuity.

Review some of the words which are descriptive of sounds:

developing
vocabulary of
descriptive
sounds

1. What sound did the turtle make as he swam in the water? (*slap*)

2. What sound do you make as you walk in puddles? (*slop*)

3. What sound does an apple make when it falls off a tree? (*plop*)

4. What sound do you make when you walk in your daddy's slippers? (*flap*)

5. What sound does the rain make on the window? (*patter*)

6. What sound does a balloon make when it breaks? (*pop*)

As the children respond freely, the teacher should list their responses; or she may write these responses in random order on the board ·or place flash cards in the pocket chart. As she asks the questions again, the children find the correct "sound" word.

Workbook page 14 follows this lesson.

Enrichment

providing
enrichment
activities

Poem: Lindsay, Vachel, "The Little Turtle," in *Anthology of Children's Literature*, Houghton Mifflin.

Story: De Huff, Elizabeth W., "The Fox and the Turtle," adapted from *Taytay's Tales,* Harcourt, Brace.

Page 33 — Introduction of b

Building Linguistic Skills

b in various positions.

Introduction

teaching
rhythm through
nursery rhymes

Use one or several nursery rhymes to demonstrate the rhythm, and at the same time, a strong /b/ sound: "Baa, Baa, Black Sheep,"

"Bow-wow-wow, Whose Dog Art Thou?" "Little Bo-Peep," or "Bye, Baby Bunting."

Procedure

1. As the children recite these rhymes, exaggerate the position of your lips, and then call attention to their position but the lack of any sound. Put **bow** on the board if you have used that nursery rhyme, or **baa**, etc. Say the word, moving your hand under it so they can see the vowels immediately following the **b**. If you must isolate **b**, remember that no voice sound accompanies **b** except when it is used with a vowel.

introducing the **b** phoneme

This may be learned as a jingle:

"Baby, balloons, button, and bow
All begin with a **b**, you know."

2. Make balloons with the following words for the flannel board. Draw balloons on the board and put the words in them if a flannel board is not available:

bat	big	cob	barn	bump
bad	but	stab	Bob	
bed	rob	ball	crab	
beg	rib	bled	bend	

As the words are read by the children, they can be used in sentences, or in answer to questions such as: "Which word means to steal? Which one is a toy? a home for animals?" (The teacher may use any device to maintain interest.)

developing vocabulary

3. Have the children close their eyes. Remove one word, or erase it. Have the children look at the list and try to guess which word was removed. The one who guesses correctly can remove the next word.

4. Direct the children to shut their eyes. Say a word and have them listen for the initial, medial, or terminal sounds, as: "What is the middle sound in **sob**? What is the last sound in **bled**? What are the first two letter sounds in **crab**?"

recognizing the initial, medial, and terminal sounds in words

5. Encourage the children to think of their own words beginning with **b**. Words with unfamiliar elements, such as in **bottle, button, berry, basket,** and **box** may be listed on the board.

6. Have the children open their books to page 33. Review by saying **balloon**, then have the children read all the words in the yellow block (words with /b/ as the initial sound).

Ask the children to look at the words in the green block. Ask where the letter **b** and the sound /b/ appears in all these words. (*at the end*) Ask the children to read the words aloud. Have words that you think are unfamiliar to your children used in sentences. Ask the pupils to find three words in the green block that both begin and end with /b/. (*bib, bulb,* and *Bob*)

Words in the blue block have two consonants before the vowel. Help the children to read these words and to use them in sentences. Ask the children to find and say aloud a two-syllable word in the blue block. (*number*)

providing
dictation
practice

7. Dictate words to be written on the board. Use the words from the previous list and from the list in the child's text:

ban	bond	tub
bar	bun	cab
Ben	bug	cub
best	bulb	hub

exercises for
independent
work

Suggestions for Further Activities

1. Have the children find pictures of words that begin with **b** in magazines. Give the children a definite number of pictures to find— four or six.

2. Have them illustrate four (or six or eight) of the **b** words from the textbook.

3. Children enjoy making booklets. Staple folded paper together to make eight pages. Print an initial consonant on each page and have the children either illustrate the consonant with crayon or find pictures of it in magazines.

making
booklets

4. Put funny phrases on the board, and have the children make booklets. Here are some examples:

a rat in a hat
a clown on a ball
the dog in a wagon
a cat in a tub

Workbook pages 15, 16, and 17 follow this lesson.

Enrichment

providing
enrichment

Poem: Brown, B. C., "Jonathan Bing," in *Anthology of Children's Literature,* Houghton Mifflin.

Page 34 — The terminal le

phoneme-
grapheme
relationships

Building Linguistic Skills

The two-syllable words resulting from the addition of the **le** phoneme to familiar phoneme-grapheme patterns.

Introduction

Review /b/ briefly, putting *bulb, bump,* and *bog* on the board. Add *bottle* to the list and give a child an opportunity to respond.

reviewing the **b** phoneme

Procedure

If no child recognizes the word, pronounce **bottle** and have the class repeat it. Pronounce these words slowly, with an exaggerated sound of the syllables: **little, apple, rattle, sniffle, waffle, rumble, saddle, tumble, puddle, settle.**

introducing the terminal **le** phoneme

Put these words on the board and have the children read them. Call attention to the double letters after the vowel and before the **le.** If there is only one consonant before **le,** the consonant is doubled before **le** (apple). If there are two consonants (tumble), there is no need to double the consonant.

Dictate the following words for spelling:

providing words for dictation

> bottle
> tumble
> saddle
> apple
> stumble

Use the words in context, either on the board or by making phrase cards:

a little car	a glass bottle
tumble down	the pans rattle
a red apple	stumble up the step
the dogs battle	a ruffle on her dress
a little apple	the waffle is hot
the big car rumbles	in the saddle
a mud puddle	fumble the ball

Duplicating Master No. 9 can be used here.

Page 35 — The Little Sled

Introduction

Discuss the illustration, including the season. Ask, "How do you know it is winter?" (*snow, clothing, etc.*) "How do the boys look?" (*worried*) "Why?" (*The sled is going too fast.*) "What other way can you ride on a sled?" (*lying down, etc.*) "How do the boys steer their sleds?" (*with their feet*)

drawing conclusions from an illustration

Guiding Reading for Comprehension

checking comprehension

Have a child find and read the title. Ask, "Who are the children?" (*Ben and Bob*) Have them find the word in the second sentence which has an **a** changed by an **r**. Call on a child to read the word. (*started*) For the third sentence, ask what the sled started to do, and where it went. (*run, down a hill*) Have the three sentences read aloud.

building suspense to motivate reading

In the second thought unit, have the children find and read the two-syllable word. (*faster*) Ask, "What did Bob and Ben do?" (*held on*) Direct them to read the last line to find out who was talking. (*Bob*) "What did he say?" (*stop the sled*) Have the last unit read aloud. Ask the class what they think happened next; accept all of the suggestions.

Page 36 — The Little Sled (*conclusion*)

Introduction

developing awareness of safety

Discuss the picture for the conclusion. Stress the importance of safety—sliding where it is safe, learning to steer, etc.

Guiding Reading for Comprehension

checking comprehension

Have the children read the first sentence; then ask them what the sled hit. (*a bump*) Ask, "What happened to Bob and Ben?"(*fell from the sled*) Guide the children to read the next three sentences. Ask them if the sled stopped. What words tell them? (*did not*) Ask what happened to the sled. (*ran into the red barn*) In the next sentence ask, "What happened to the sled when it ran into the barn?" (*bent*) "What happened to the barn?" (*dented*) In the last sentence ask, "What happened to Bob and Ben?" (*got wet*) Have the entire page read aloud.

Continue the safety discussion for this story. Encourage free expression of the children's own experiences.

Suggestions for Further Activities

creative drawing

1. Suggest free creative drawing of each child's own experiences in snow. Encourage children to tell the story that their picture illustrates. This can be done orally, as they show their pictures to the class, or again they can be dictated to the teacher who can print or type them.

2. Have the children fill in the missing letter in the following words that you put on the board. Be sure to check to see that they

can read them when they have finished. Letter boxes are useful in this type of exercise.

b__ttle	app____	se____le
l__ttle	waff____	sni____le
r__ffle	st____ble	ri____le

Duplicating Master No. 10 follows this lesson.

Workbook page 18 may be used here. Workbook page 19 is a vocabulary test.

S*U*P*E*R Book No. 30, *Martin Crumpet*, follows this lesson.

providing independent work

★

Enrichment

Poems: Aldis, Dorothy, "Ice," in *The Golden Flute*, Hubbard and Babbitt, Day.

Bush, Joselyn, "The Little Red Sled," in *Arbuthnot Anthology of Children's Literature*, Scott, Foresman.

Miller, Nellie Burget, "The Snow," in *The Golden Flute*, Hubbard and Babbitt, Day.

Turner, Nancy Byrd, "The Best Time of All," in *Anthology of Children's Literature*, Houghton Mifflin.

Wilkins, Alice, "Snow," in *The Golden Flute*, Hubbard and Babbitt, Day.

Wynne, Annette, "Song of the Snowflakes," in *The Golden Flute*, Hubbard and Babbitt, Day.

providing poems for enrichment

Page 37 — The initial and terminal k

Building Linguistic Skills

/k/ and the rule that usually **k** is used with **i** and **e**, and **c** with **a, o,** and **u**.

phoneme-grapheme relationships

Introduction

Show either a large mounted picture of a king or the illustration on page 37. Ask who this is. Print the response (*king*) on the board and have the children pronounce it. Explain that there are two letters that spell the same sound. (Recall **c** in **cat**.)

introducing the **k** phoneme

Procedure

1. /k/ as an initial sound:
   a) Have the children pronounce the following words after you as you write them on the board:

providing visual discrimination exercises

33

kitten	Kenneth	kiss	kilt
kettle	kitchen	keg	kept

Have the children find and draw a line around the vowels following the **k**. Call attention to the fact that they are all **e** or **i** and explain that **a, o,** and **u** usually follow **c**.

distinguishing between the **c** and **k** graphemes

b) Pronounce the following words and have the children identify the vowel sound. After they have determined the vowel, have them name the initial consonant in each word:

cat	kitten	kitchen	custard
cup	copy	carriage	candy
keg	cuddle	kept	kiss

To make a game of this exercise, draw two trains on the board. Put **c** on the engine of one, and **k** on the engine of the other. After identifying the vowel sound in a word, a child goes to the correct train and puts his initials in it (he is riding on the train). A more permanent device can be made by cutting two trains out of oaktag and making slits for windows. Put the initial consonant on a small piece of oaktag and attach it to the engine with a paper clip. (This makes it possible to use the device for a variety of phonetic situations.) Each child has a small colored "ticket" with his initials on it. When he gives the correct response, he inserts his ticket in a slit, thereby proving he can ride on the train.

playing a game to reinforce the **c** and **k** graphemes

c) Play an active game by having the children stand. Read a list similar to the above to them; the children stoop when they hear a word which begins with **k** (has **i** or **e** as a vowel sound), and stand when they hear the words beginning with **c** (**a, o, u** vowel sounds).

d) Make a chart on the board and dictate words at random. Have the children put them in the proper column, either under **c** or **k**.

cat	kit	kitten
cup	cot	cat
kill	cub	keg
cost	kilt	cob
cast	kept	kiss

recognizing **k** in a terminal position

2. **k** as a terminal consonant after **s, l,** and **r**:

a) Say **milk** and have someone tell where he hears the **k** sound. Call on a child to write it on the board. Follow with **silk, task, mask, risk,** and **dark**.

b) Have the children read the words on page 37 that have **k** at the beginning and that have **k** following a consonant other than **c**.

3. Do an exercise similar to (d) in exercise 1 above, adding **k** as a terminal sound:

c	k	-k

Use the same list, but include *mask, task, risk, silk, milk, dark, park,* and *mark.*

Workbook page 20 follows this lesson.
Duplicating Master No. 11 can be used here.

Page 38 — A poem: Mitten, mitten

Introduction

This poem creates a picture of a little kitten on a mat.

Procedure

1. Have the children read the poem silently.
2. Ask for the name of the animal—cat or kitten. Ask what the children think the kitten looks like. Bring out, if the children do not, that he has paws like mittens and is wearing a mitten on one paw.
3. Ask for two pairs of rhyming words. (*kitten, mitten; cat, mat*)
4. Have the children read the poem in unison; then two or three may read it to the group for enjoyment.
Workbook page 21 follows this lesson.

Page 39 — Words ending with ck

Building Linguistic Skills

The rule that usually the **ck** phoneme follows a short vowel that has no other consonant following it.

Introduction

Direct the children's attention to the picture of the **sock.** Ask what the last sound is. (*k*) Do they hear any sound after the vowel before the **k** as they do in **milk** or **dark**? (*no*) Explain that when the **k** sound follows the vowel and comes at the end of a word, we use **ck** for the sound. Have the children read the **ck** words in the text.

Procedure

1. Pronounce a word from the list in the book and have the children listen to decide whether there is another sound between the vowel and the **k** sound.

distinguishing between **k** and **ck** graphemic patterns

2. Put the word **milk** on the board and call attention to the **k** after l in **milk** and the **ck** after **a** in **sack**, etc. This rule must be repeated many times for mastery. Use the list on page 39.

3. Put **k** and **ck** on the board, or have the children fold writing paper and put **k** and **ck** at the top:

k	ck

Dictate **mask, tick, truck, ask, lock, peck, dark,** and have the children write them under the correct headings. Use also:

desk	task	rack	park
risk	pick	milk	luck
pack	dusk	duck	lark
dock	silk	rock	sock

Suggestions for Further Activities

providing further activities for discrimination

1. For more difficult experiences, put on the board lines such as "A tisket, a tasket, a little yellow basket," "Lucy Locket lost her pocket," and "Five, six, pick up sticks." Have the children find the **k** sounds, read the words, and develop the sentences. Nursery rhymes can then be said in unison or by individuals.

exercises for independent work

2. Have the children complete words either from the board or on a duplicated paper. Give them the initial sound, example:

sil___, mas___, la___, etc.

3. Have the children add **ck** to the following initial sounds and illustrate them.

ro___	ta___	ne___	ki___
so___	du___	si___	sti___

Duplicating Master No. 12 gives additional practice with the **ck** digraph and may be used following this lesson.

Page 40 — A poem — The Little Black Dog

Introduction

Before having the children open their books to this poem, read the poem, "The Animal Store," to them. (See the Bibliography, page 42.)

Guiding Reading for Recognition of Rhythm and Rhyme

recognizing rhyming words

1. Tell the children that this is also a poem, and have them read the title. Ask how the boy and the dog are having fun together. Let the pupils discuss things they like to do outdoors.

2. Put the words **pick, park,** and **black** on the chalkboard. Review what makes words that rhyme; then have the children read the poem silently to find words that rhyme with the words on the chalkboard. (*stick, bark,* and *back*) Working with these words ahead of time will mean that the children will be able to read the poem aloud with greater ease. Familiarity with these words will also make it easier for them to read the poem with a sense of rhythm.

3. Ask the children to locate the first period, then to reread the whole sentence to themselves. Choose an individual to read it aloud.

4. Do the same with the second sentence. Call attention to the fact that this sentence does not end with a period. Have two or three children read the entire poem aloud.

Workbook page 22 can be used here.
S*U*P*E*R Book No. 31, *Buttons the Clown*, can be used here.

Page 41 — Words ending in nk

Building Linguistic Skills

phoneme-grapheme relationships

The terminal blend **nk.**

Introduction

introducing the terminal **nk** phonemic pattern

Call attention to the illustration. Have the children say the words **pink, drink** (illustration) after you, prolonging the terminal sound. Ask if they ever had a pink drink—a pink soda. Allow time for discussion of personal experiences.

Procedure

building
auditory
discrimination
of **ck** and **nk**
phonemic
patterns

1. Have the children repeat after you—**bank, ink, tank, sunk.** Emphasize in your pronunciation the difference of the **n** when followed by **k.** Point out that the sound is rather nasal in quality, coming through the nose. Say paired words, such as **sink** and **sick, bank** and **back,** emphasizing the **nk.** Now say pairs, and ask which (first or second) had the **nk** ending. Here are some possibilities:

tack - tank	sink - sick	pink - pick
hank - hack	tick - ink	sank - sack
spank - stack	wick - wink	rank - rack

enriching
vocabulary

2. Have the children read the words in the book. As each word is read, ask a child to use it in a sentence. Encourage them to use all the meanings of such words as: **tank**—an army tank, an oil tank, a fish tank; **sink**—the kitchen sink, to sink; **bank**—to put in a bank, a savings bank, a river bank. Time spent on enriching a child's vocabulary is never wasted. It may be well to note here that we do not teach the meaning of a word only as it is to be used in the story. Therefore, it is not necessary to drill on the word as it is to be found in context. As the phoneme-grapheme patterns are presented and analyzed, the word meanings are developed.

exercises for
dictation

3. Dictate some of the words from page 41, using them in phrases or sentences, and have the children write them. The entire group may write them on paper while individual children write the words on the board. Here are some suggested sentences and words for this exercise.

bank: "I put my money in the bank." **bank**
sink: "Did the boat sink?" **sink**
link: "Each part of a chain is a link." **link**
ink: "We use ink in pens." **ink**
sank: "The rock sank to the bottom of the lake." **sank**
drink: "Did you drink your milk?" **drink**
rink: "We skate at the rink." **rink**
tank: "We have a tank for hot water in the basement." **tank**
mink: "A mink is a small animal whose fur is very valuable."
  mink
wink: "Let me see you wink." **wink**

Suggestions for Further Activities

1. Give the children a duplicated sheet with pictures (Duplicating Master No. 13). Have them complete the words under each picture. For example:

2. Put the following sentences on a duplicated sheet or use Duplicating Master No. 14, and have the children draw a line around the correct word and put the word on the line.

further exercises for discrimination of terminal blends

Ann's drink is _____.
          pink   pick

The rock _____ in the water.
      sank   sack

The _____ wall is red.
 brink   brick

Put _____ in the pen.
  silk   ink

Workbook page 23 follows this lesson.

Pages 42 and 43 — The Black Cow

of

Introduction

In discussing the picture, bring out that this is the country. Point out how it differs from the city. This is an excellent opportunity to enrich the children's knowledge of both the city and the country. Ask the children where they get their milk. Many will have no understanding beyond the milkman who delivers the milk each morning, or the local grocery store. Bring out other differences

enriching class knowledge of city and country

—the presence of trees, fields, few houses with much land, as contrasted with apartment houses and playgrounds, etc. It would be worthwhile here to have good mounted illustrations of skyscrapers or city traffic, as well as pictures of farms, country roads, etc.

taking field trip
or using films
related to
the story

The ideal would be a field trip to a local farm or dairy where the children can actually see cows—see them being cared for and milked. If this is an impossibility, as it is for many areas today, there are several good films available, such as "Uncle Jim's Dairy Farm," loaned by the National Dairy Council, and others as suggested on page 101 of this Teacher's Edition.

Sets of posters are available from the National Dairy Council that explain the steps from the time the cow is milked, through the taking of the milk to the local milk depot, where most farmers take their milk, then transporting the milk via tank train or tank truck to the city where it is homogenized, pasteurized, bottled, etc., at the milk plant, and lastly, delivered by truck to homes and stores.

developing
understanding
of milk
processing

Stress the importance of cleanliness of the cow, and everything that comes in contact with the milk.

Guiding Reading for Comprehension

reading the
title to learn
about the story

The title could include the farm, the boy, the cat, or the cow. Have the children read the title to find out what the story is about. (the black cow) Continue the silent reading to find out the name of the boy, (Bob) the new word in the second line (kept), what Bob does to the cow, (rubs her back and neck) and how the cow feels toward Bob. (will not harm) Follow with reading aloud. Ask the children why they think the cat is there.

making
inferences
from pictures

From the picture, have the children identify what Bob is doing. Do they think this is a big farm or a little one? (little—one cow, milked by hand; a large farm would have many cows milked by machines) Now have them tell why the cat is there. Ask what the cat wants. (milk) Say, "Yes, it wants a drink of milk." Put the phrase on the board, moving your hand under it as you reread it, and then have a child read it. Have another child frame of. Ask what letter usually spells /v/. (the letter v) Tell the children that they will need to remember that in this little word, /v/ is spelled or represented by the letter f. Ask the children to find of on page 43.

introducing
the special
word of

Direct the children to read the first two sentences, and then ask, What does Bob want? (to get milk) What can Bob do? (milk a cow) Have both sentences read aloud.

checking
comprehension

In the next sentence have the children find the cat's name and color. (Tab, tan) Ask what the cat does. Be sure they read the second sentence to find out. (begs) Direct the children to read the last sentence silently before reading the three sentences together. The last three sentences can be read by three children, then by one child. The entire story can be reread aloud by several children.

40

Discuss further what kind of animal a cow is. (*farm animal rather than a zoo animal or pet*) Then discuss what kind of animal a cat is. (*pet, or farm animal*) How does the cat help the farmer? (*catches mice in the barn*)

Suggestions for Further Activities

learning about categorizing animals

1. This lesson should be used to enrich the child's background, either through further study of country life, or through categorizing animals as zoo animals, pets, wild animals, or farm animals. A series of lessons can include the habits of each type, as well as recognition of familiar animals and their characteristics. Some of the categories might include animals with similar coverings: fur, hair, feathers, scales, shells, etc.; or animals with similar methods of moving: four legs, two legs and wings, six legs, many legs, no legs, fins, etc.; or homes: nest, burrow, hole in tree, cave.

exercises for independent work

2. Many independent activities can be suggested, such as, making scrapbooks of animals by categories, or experience charts. Some examples are:

I am an elephant.
I am very big.
I have a long trunk to help lift big logs.

The farmer has horses and cows.
The cows give us milk.
The horses help pull the farm wagon.

using riddles to develop vocabulary

3. The following riddles can be used orally:

I am a small animal.
I say, "Quack, quack."
I am a good swimmer.
What animal am I? (*a duck*)

I live in a nest.—I am a _____. (*bird*)
I live in a barn.—I begin with c. (*cow*)
I lay eggs.—I begin with h. (*hen*)

4. Have the children complete words to make the names of farm animals:

c__w   pi__
ca__   __en
d__g   d__ck

Use Duplicating Master No. 15 to make scrapbooks.
Workbook pages 24, 25, and 26 follow this lesson.
S*U*P*E*R Book No. 32, *Hiccups*, can be used here.

Enrichment

Animal Tale: "The Little Red Hen and the Grain of Wheat," in Hutchinson's *Chimney Corner Stories*, Putnam's.

Poems: Arbuthnot, May Hill, "My Dog," by Marchette Chute, "The Animal Store," Rachel Field, "The Buccaneer," Nancy Byrd Turner, and "The Hairy Dog," Herbert Asquith, are all in *Time for Poetry,* Scott Foresman.

Mitchell, Lucy Sprague, "The Farmer Tries to Sleep," in *Here and Now Story Book,* Dutton.

Stevenson, R. L., "The Cow," in *A Child's Garden of Verses,* Oxford.

<table>
<tr><td>providing
stories for
enrichment</td></tr>
</table>

Stories: Beatty, John Y., *Story Pictures of Farm Animals,* Beckley Cardy.

Brown, Margaret Wise, *Baby Animals,* Random.

Brown, Margaret Wise, *Country Noisy Book,* Scott, Foresman.

Hader, Berta and Elmer, *Cock-a-Doodle Doo,* Macmillan.

Hader, Berta and Elmer, *Farmer in the Dell,* Macmillan.

Lenski, Lois, *The Little Farm,* Oxford.

Meeks, Esther K., *Friendly Farm Animals,* Follett.

Mitchell, Lucy Sprague, "Eben's Cows," and "The Milk's Journey," in *Here and Now Story Book,* Dutton.

Pages 44 and 45 — Introduction of signal e

Building Linguistic Skills

phoneme-grapheme relationships

A careful and thorough presentation of the signal **e** results in a child's being able to read many new words. The following suggested introduction should be adapted to meet the class situation.

Introduction

Explain that many children in the class are not called by their real names, but by their "nicknames," or short names. Robert's real name is Robert, but his friends and his family call him "Bobby" or "Bob," which is a short name. Sue's real name is Susan, which is her long name, but we often call her "Sue." Tom's real name is Thomas, and Ned's is Edward. So most of us have a long way of saying our names, but we also have a short way that we use very often. So it is with the vowel sounds.

introducing short and long a

At this point, either point to **a** in the alphabet or write **a** on the board. Ask the children for the name of this letter (they are entirely familiar with the alphabet by now). Say, "Yes, that **a** (letter name) is the real name, like our real names; so we call it the *long* sound of the letter. Ask for the sound of **a** they have heard in **can.** Explain that this is like our short names. It is still a sound of **a,** but does not say its real name, so we call it a *short* sound of **a.**

42

Procedure

1. Explain that there are several ways to tell when the **a** is long. Today we will learn the easiest way. Take the flash card **can** (or print it on the board). Have a child read the word. Add **e,** using a small card, or add it to the word on the board. Call their attention to what has been added to **can.** Explain that we call this a "signal **e**" because it signals the sound represented by the other vowel in monosyllabic words. The **e** does not represent a sound itself. It is silent. It serves as a signal that the other vowel usually changes from a short sound to a long sound. Use flash cards **mat, rat, man, tam,** and **hat,** following the same procedure.

2. Dictate one of the above words and have a child write it on the board. Then call on a second child to change it. For example, if the first child puts **fat** on the board, a second child will change it to **fate.** Don't have the second child print the entire word, but merely add the **e** to the original word.

3. Call attention to the first eight words on **page 44;** discuss them with the children. Ask what kind of vowel they hear in **can, cane,** etc., so that they will not only change the words and read them correctly, but will also become completely familiar with the terms "short" and "long" in this situation.

4. Now dictate words at random, and the children must discern whether there is a long or short vowel, and therefore whether they must remember the **e.**

Here is a suggested list:

presenting the long **a** phoneme

changing short **a** to long **a** with signal **e**

providing exercises in auditory discrimination

words for dictation practice

man	stab	bale	fade
mane	state	bat	cast
game	late	same	hate
tame	lap	ram	drab
pan	snap	rate	date
pane	map	came	had

Several children can be involved simultaneously if you have a group at the board and give each child a different word to print. This also eliminates any possibility of copying.

5. Have the children open their books again and look at page 45. Call the children's attention to the words **car** and **care.** Help the children become aware that although signal or final **e** is added to **car,** the result is not **cāre.** The **r** changes the vowel so that **ar** sounds like **air.**

ar and **are** words

Help the children read all the words. Ask them to use the words that end in **e** in sentences to clarify meanings.

Suggestions for Further Activities

Put the following words on the board, have the children add **e** and illustrate the resulting word. As you give this assignment, give the children an opportunity to discover the resulting word and discuss its meaning. For example, the word **mate** suggests socks that go together, or shoes that go together. A **mare** may not be within the child's understanding vocabulary.

can___	at___	pan___
mat___	cap___	mar___

Page 46 — Further experience with long a words

Procedure

1. The additional words on page 46 can be used for rapid drill around the class, or in any way that the teacher chooses. It is important also that the teacher call attention to the **k** in **make, sake,** etc. After a long vowel, only the **k** is used. Here is an excellent opportunity for developing vocabulary; have a child read a word, and then use it in a sentence. You may also put a sentence on the board, have the children read it silently (allowing time for silent study here is essential), and then call on a child to read it orally. Have the child, or another child, locate the "signal **e**," underline the word, and pronounce it. (*Note*: **sail, tail, hair,** and **bear** are not used for these exercises.)

Here are a few suggestions:

Tell the **tale** of Rags and Tags. (Here you explain the difference in meaning between **tale** and **tail.**)

The men shot up a **flare.** (Again, explanation of the meaning is important.)

This rug was on **sale.** (If a child gives the meaning of **sail,** clarify it; otherwise, it is not necessary to refer to **sail.**)

The **hare** can hop and run fast. (different from **hair**)

The sun tans **bare** legs and backs. (different from **bear**)

The **mare** has a black mane.

2. Select from the flash cards the following words: **can, at, rat, cap, mat, fat, car, star, spar,** and **far.** Put them with the long **a** words for rapid discriminatory drill.

3. Select words from the list for the children to write on the board. Call on as many children as board space will permit, and give each child his own word to write. Avoid having all the children write the same word.

44

Suggestions for Further Activities

1. After these words have been dictated for spelling and the children have a good basic understanding, a more difficult dictation lesson would include such words as **ball, saw, pan, black,** and **far,** as well as the long **a** words. Give the children an opportunity to recall other linguistic rules and make fine discriminations.

making fine auditory discriminations

2. List these words on the board. For independent work, have the children add **e,** read, and illustrate the new words.

exercises for independent work

| can | mar | tam | Sal |
| cap | man | at | Sam |

3. Active games can be played with flash cards. Let one child hold a flash card so that all can see it; call on a child to read it. Call another child (a signal) with **e** card to stand beside the first child and add his **e** to the word. Have the child read—**cane.**

These words can be used:

can	at	rat	cap	par	hat	fad
mat	fat	gap	pan	ball	war	gall
car	bar	bass	slat	far	Sam	stall
mar	star	tall	pal	tam	man	

Note: In cases where the word ends in **ll** or **ss,** direct the child with the **e** to cover the final **l** or **s.**

Duplicating Master No. 16 can be used here.

Workbook page 27 follows this lesson.

Page 47 — Black Mane and Tim

Introduction

This story follows a farm theme and gives an additional opportunity for the children to learn about life on a farm. The illustration should be used as a basis for such a discussion. Ask such questions as, "What animals do you see? (*rabbit, horse*) What is another name for rabbit? (*hare*) Where are these animals? (*on a farm*) Who lives in the building? (*animals*) What kind of building is it? (*barn*) Why do they have a fence?" (*to hold animals*) These questions will recall previous facts about the farm.

continuing to learn about farm life

Guiding Reading for Comprehension

Have the children study the title, and then have one child read it aloud. Ask who "Black Mane" is and why the horse is so named. (*black as slate*) Ask who Tim must be. (*hare*) Have the children read

checking comprehension

silently to find out what kind of horse Black Mane is. (*pet mare*) At this point, if the word **mare** has not been discussed in a previous lesson, it will be necessary either to find out if the children know the meaning of the word, or to explain that a mare is a female (mother) horse. Have the children read the second line to find the word that tells how black her mane is. Call on a child to describe Black Mane in his own words. Then have another child read the two lines orally.

Tell the children that the next line describes Tim. Have them find the words that describe (use this term) him or tell what he looks like. (*small, brown*) The last line tells what they did together. (*ate the grass*) Have the entire page read orally. Before turning the page, ask if the children think Black Mane and Tim are friends.

making inferences from the story

Page 48 — Black Mane and Tim (*continued*)

Introduction

interpreting picture clues

In presenting this picture, emphasize that very few snakes are harmful. The hare is small and frightened.

Guiding Reading for Comprehension

Have the class point to the word **snake.** How many times can they find it on the page? (4) "How did the snake look at Tim?" (*stare*) "What words describe the snake?" (*big, black*) Have the page read orally. Ask the children what they think will happen next. Suggest a happy ending if they tend toward only unhappy conclusions.

drawing conclusions

The teacher must use her own judgment on the number of questions she should ask during the guided reading part of the lesson. For an average group or better, too many questions will slow the lesson down. Questions are included here to meet the teacher's needs, but she is not expected to use all of them with every group.

With most groups, this page can be used as a single unit. Have the children read the page, and then ask, "How did Tim get Black Mane to run fast?" (*He told her to.*) Have the page read aloud. Work for expression, particularly in quotations.

oral reading for expression

Page 49 — Black Mane and Tim
(*conclusion*)

Guiding Reading for Comprehension

Have the first three sentences read to find out how tall the gate was. (*as tall as the mare*) After the children have read and responded to the thought question, ask what Black Mane asked Tim to do. (*help*) This procedure gives a question before the children read: they are reading to find out. Then, after they have finished reading, ask another question to check their comprehension.

The next three sentences present the second situation where the *ed* added to the base word does not result in a two-syllable word. For the sake of the story, it is necessary to include it here. Have the children read the fourth line silently. Then call on a child to read it aloud. Through common usage, he will probably read it correctly. However, if he does not, correct him by saying, "That *is* how it looks, because that is the way it is spelled, but how do we say it?" Some child in the group will undoubtedly pronounce it correctly. If no one knows, it will be necessary to tell them.

checking comprehension

reviewing pronunciations of the ed suffix

Have the children read the next sentence silently; then orally. Have them read the last sentence to find out how the story ends. Call on a child to read the last three sentences for continuity.

Ask the children if they liked the story. If so, try to find out why. Is it because it is an animal story, or do they like stories about horses, or is it the plot—the snake trying to get the rabbit, and the latter being rescued? Such a discussion can also help children to understand that friends working together can accomplish much. Ask, "Did the hare need the horse's help?" (*yes*) "Did the horse need the hare's help?" (*yes*) Any lesson or moral from this story should be built around this point.

developing reasons for liking the story

Here is another natural point from which to build creative stories. Show pictures of animals, or give each child a picture, and have him create his own story.

providing creative writing experiences

Duplicating Master No. 17 follows this lesson.
Workbook page 28 follows this lesson.
S*U*P*E*R Book No. 33, *A Picnic in the Park*, can be used here.

Enrichment

Beim, Lorraine and Jerrold, *Two Is a Team*, Harcourt. (An excellent book to bring out this same point—working together is the only way.)

Stories of Horses: Anderson, C. W., *Billy and Blaze*, Macmillan.
Gall, Alice Crew and Crew, Fleming, "The Song of the Little Donkey," in *Told Under the Magic Umbrella*, Macmillan.

stories of horses and rabbits for enrichment

47

Stories of Rabbits: Aesop, "The Hare and the Tortoise," in *Anthology of Children's Literature,* Houghton Mifflin.

Bailey, Carolyn Sherwin, *The Rabbit Who Wanted Red Wings,* Platt and Munk.

Young, Martha, "How Mr. Rabbit got a Good Dinner," and "The Dyeing of Mr. Rabbit," in Bailey, *Merry Tales for Children,* Platt and Munk.

Page 50 — Long e

been

Building Linguistic Skills

phoneme-
grapheme
relationships

Continuation of long vowel sounds, including terminal **e** and the **ee** digraph.

Introduction

Review the story of our long names and our short names. Put a child's name (from the class) on the board in a sentence:

Stan can run.

Have a child read it. Under it write:

teaching the
pronoun *he*

He can run fast.

Ask the children what word was used instead of repeating *Stan.* (*He*)

Procedure

introducing the
long **e**
phoneme

1. Have a child read the sentence; then have another underline **he.** Repeat **he** and ask what vowel sound the children hear. (*long e*) Ask a child to change **he** to **we** and to read the sentence. Write **me** on the board. Ask the children to say the word and tell you what vowel sound they hear. Have the children say all the two-letter words you have written that contain long **e.**

providing
exercises in
auditory
discrimination
of long **e**

2. Write **pet** on the board, and have it read. Under it write **Pete.** Explain that just as **can** became **cane** when signal **e** was added, so **pet** becomes **Pete** with the addition of signal **e.** In some regions **here** is pronounced (hēr). The children should become aware that the final **e** spells no sound.

3. Ask the children to turn to page 50 and read all the words in the yellow block.

48

4. Have the children examine the words in the green block. Ask how many **e**'s they see in each word. *(2)* Are they together? *(yes)* Explain that when two vowels come together in a word, we usually hear only one vowel sound—the long sound of the first vowel. The second vowel spells no sound. This is called a *vowel digraph*. Write a few words from the green block on the chalkboard. Ask children to read a word, to draw a line under the two **e**'s, and then to use the word in a sentence. Use many of these words in sentences to clarify the meanings. For instance, **steel** should be used correctly and not confused' with **steal**; and **deer** should not be confused with **dear**.

5. Have the children read the words in the blue block.

6. Use **been** in a sentence: *He has been here for a week.* Have the children mark all the long **e**'s, and read the sentence orally. Notice the pronunciation of **been** and explain that it is a special word which most people pronounce **bin**. Some people say **bēēn**.

introducing the special word *been*

7. Put other phrases or sentences on the board, reviewing the long and short **a** and **e**. Have the children read the sentence, then underline and pronounce the long and short vowel words.

reviewing long and short **a** and **e**

a) Pete has seen his pet.
b) Did Ann take her hat?
c) We will rake the grass.
d) He has a bat and ball to trade.
e) We need a bed for Sam.
f) The deer ran up the steep hill.
g) Make a cake for me.
h) The mare is for sale.

Suggestions for Further Activities

1. Activity 7 in the preceding section can be set up for independent work. Directions should be at the top of the paper, followed by sentences similar to those used in step 7. The children could be directed to mark words with long **e** with a green crayon, and words having long **a** with a red crayon. Duplicating Master No. 18 has a similar exercise.

2. Make a duplicated sheet with vowels missing from words. The children identify the words from the pictures and fill in the missing vowels. Duplicating Master No. 19 is a similar exercise.

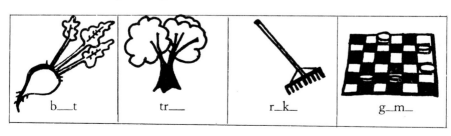

b__t   tr__   r_k_   g_m_

3. Have the children find words with **ee** on pages torn from newspapers or magazines. The children circle words and read those they can recognize.

Workbook page 29 follows this lesson.

Enrichment

The following poem can be taught.

> In the heart of a seed, buried deep, so deep,
> A dear little plant lay fast asleep.

Write the poem on a piece of oaktag and have the children frame the words with **ee** and read them.

Page 51 — Red Deer

Introduction

Discuss details of the picture. The deer eating the beets can be compared to Peter Rabbit in Mr. McGregor's garden. Bring out the childish fun in the Peter Rabbit story, and draw parallels.

Guiding Reading for Comprehension

introducing
two-line
sentences

developing
oral reading
skills

Read the title to learn the deer's name. (*Red Deer*) These stories in which the animals have names are more like the old Thornton Burgess favorites, or *Mother West Wind Stories*. The attitude of the teacher should be to maintain the tenor of such stories. Direct the children to read the first three sentences. Call their attention to a sentence that goes from one line to another. The sentence starts with a capital and ends with a period. After silent reading, ask what kind of farm it was. (*beet farm*) What word describes the deer? (*Red*) Have a child read the two-line sentence again. Have a child read the last three sentences. Be sure the last sentence is read without hesitation.

Page 52 — Red Deer (*continued*)

Guiding Reading for Comprehension

Call the children's attention to the next long sentence. This tells why the farmer has a stick. After silent reading, have the entire sentence read orally. Several children may read it for fluency. Have the children read the next two sentences silently, and then orally. Complete the page in this way.

Page 53 — Red Deer (*conclusion*)

Guiding Reading for Comprehension

There are several two-line sentences on this page. Give the children an opportunity to read these sentences silently before reading the page orally. Ask questions to review the story after they read silently. "What could the farmer see?" Say, "Put your finger on the word that tells the answer." (*antlers*) "How did Red Deer get away? Put your finger on the word that tells what Red Deer did." (*swam*) "Did the farmer hit Red Deer?" (*no*) "Will Red Deer return to the farm?" (*no*) "Where will he get his food?" (*forest*) Have the page read in thought units by several children.

locating
answers
to questions

Discuss Red Deer and what he eats in the forest, his speed in swimming and running, his slim legs and great antlers. Bring out how nature has equipped Red Deer to protect himself.

A natural conclusion to this story would be a discussion of taking care of animals. The children will be familiar with taking care of pets, but here you may bring out how we take care of animals in the forest. Also discuss how these animals find ways to protect themselves. Bring out the fact that the deer hid because it was afraid. Animals are often afraid of people.

Duplicating Master No. 20 can be used as a comprehension check for the story.

Enrichment

providing
enrichment
stories

Jackson, Kathryn and Byron, *Big Farmer Big and Little Farmer Little,* Simon.

Lenski, Lois, *The Little Farm,* Oxford.

Page 54 — Vowel digraph ea

Building Linguistic Skills

phoneme-
grapheme
relationships

Continuation of long e spelled **ea.**

51

Introduction

Review the vowel digraph rule, recalling that when two vowels come together we usually hear the long sound of the first vowel. Put **see** on the board, then—*He can see me.* Under **see,** put **sea.** *The sea is big.* Explain that **see** and **sea** sound the same but have different meanings. Have a child read the second sentence, and then clarify the meaning, if necessary.

Procedure

1. After you have put the following list of words on the board, have one child draw a line around the vowel digraphs in each. Then have another pronounce the first word, and another repeat the vowel sound he hears, telling whether it is long or short.

feet	feat
meet	meat
peek	peak
beet	beat

Use the words in sentences to show their meanings.

2. Use the books to read many words containing long **ea.** Have the children find the words in answer to such directions as those listed below:

Find the name of an animal who swims. (*seal*)
Find another name for the ocean. (*sea*)
Find the name of a vegetable. (*bean* or *pea*)
Find something to eat. (*meat*)
Find a part of our body. (*ear*)
Find a word that tells how we should keep our room and our desk. (*neat*)
Find what we sit on. (*seat*)
Find a word we use to be polite. (*please*)
Find what Santa Claus has. (*beard*)
Find something on a tree. (*leaf*)
Find something we get from the sun. (*heat*)
Find another word for jump. (*leap*)
Find what we are learning to do. (*read*)

3. Use flash cards with the words from page 54 to drill the class on all the words. Two teams may be formed. Keep score of the right responses to see who wins. Many uses of flash cards may be found. They may be put in the card holder and questions like those included above used. Individuals may be called on, and then two children can be chosen. The question (or word) is given and the two will race to see who can find it first.

4. A word may be shown on the flash card and the children called on to put a rhyming word on the board.

Suggestions for Further Activities

1. Correlate with writing by having the children copy the following list and mark the vowels as *long* or *short*:

exercises for independent work

here	me
bed	meat
seam	net
see	east
fell	end
feat	eat

2. Have the children illustrate their own animal booklets. Use Duplicating Master No. 21.

making animal booklets

a black seal	a bumble bee	a little hare
a brown deer	a green snake	a tame mare
a dear little cat	a beast of the forest	

3. Give the children a sheet like the following. Have them complete the words. Tell them to use pages 50 and 54 for reference.

__ee___	__ea___
__ee___	__ea___
__ee___	__ea___
__ee___	__ea___
__ee___	__ea___

4. Give the children these simple riddles. The answers will be found on page 54. Have them write the correct answer on the lines.

using riddles to develop vocabulary

It is deep.
It is big.
It is wet.
It is the s__. (*sea*)

It can be a mare.
It can be a cow.
It can be a deer in the forest.
It is a b_____. (*beast*)

It falls from a tree.
It is brown in winter.
It can be red and yellow.
It is a l_____. (*leaf*)

It is in a cup.
It is hot.
We drink it.
It is t__. (*tea*)

Duplicating Master No. 22 duplicates these riddles. Duplicating Master No. 23 also follows this lesson.

Note: Many of these suggested activities will be needed only for the slower learners.

Workbook page 30 can be used here or after page 57.

Enrichment

Story: Asbjornsen, P. C., "The Lad Who Went to the North Wind," in *Anthology of Children's Literature,* Houghton Mifflin.
Hoff, Syd, *Sammy, the Seal,* Harper.

providing enrichment activities

Poem: Stevenson, R. L., "At the Seaside," in *A Child's Garden of Verses,* Oxford.

Page 55 — Don and Nell Dig Clams

using pictures
to develop
story
background

Introduction

The scene in this illustration may be completely unfamiliar to many children. It may be necessary for the teacher to repeat that clams are shellfish and that they are dug out of the mud under the water. Allow the children to ask questions.

Guiding Reading for Comprehension

checking
comprehension

Have the title read to discover whom the story is about and what they are doing. Direct the children to read the first two sentences to find out where this story takes place. (*at the sea*) After the class has read this thought unit, ask why Nell wanted clams. (*to eat*)

The second thought unit describes what the children need. (*a bucket and a rake*) After finding the names of the tools, have each sentence read orally. Strive for fluency with two-line sentences.

Page 56 — Don and Nell Dig Clams (*continued*)

Special Word I

I

introducing the
pronoun *I*

As the long i sound has not yet been introduced, the word **I** is treated as a special word. It will be included with the long i group, but is needed at this time in the story. It should be enough to call the attention of the group to the **I** at the bottom of the page. When a child has identified it by letter name, tell him that this is the word we use when speaking of ourselves. Have the children find **I** in the story, and call on a child to read the sentence aloud.

Guiding Reading for Comprehension

reading to
answer
questions

Ask, "Did the children get any clams?" (*yes*) How will they cook them?" (*steam*) Allow time for silent reading to find the answers. "In order to get steam, what must the children do?" (*heat water*)

54

"Who will heat the water?" (*Nell*) Follow the silent reading with oral reading. Call attention to the one-syllable pronunciation of *steamed*.

Page 57 — Don and Nell Dig Clams (*conclusion*)

Introduction

enjoying the picture

Allow time for enjoyment of the picture.

Guiding Reading for Comprehension

Ask, "Who is talking first? What did she say?" (*Nell, Please pass me a clam.*) Have the words in the quotations read orally. Ask what the children did next, and have the words read orally. (*ate clams*)

In the next thought unit, ask how many clams each child ate. (*Nell, 10; Don, 15*)

Finally, ask how they felt after they had eaten. (*full*) Have the entire page read orally.

relating personal experiences to the story

As this may be a new experience for many children, the story can be reread for pleasure. Also, children can be encouraged to talk about their own experiences at the beach or at a lake.

Suggestions for Further Activities

1. Have the children illustrate their own experiences at the beach, or camping, etc.

2. Encourage creative writing at every opportunity. Here the children may compose two- or three-sentence stories to accompany their pictures. These stories can be written by the children, with the teacher assisting with words that the children cannot spell.

creative writing exercise

3. If a story seems difficult for any child at this time, try having him make up only a title to accompany his picture. He will begin to grasp the difference between a sentence and a title.

Workbook page 31 follows this lesson.

Duplicating Master No. 24 can be used here.

S*U*P*E*R Book No. 34, *The Easter Egg Hunt*, follows this lesson.

Enrichment

Story: McCloskey, Robert, *One Morning in Maine*, Viking.

Poems: Field, Rachel, "I'd Like to Be a Lighthouse," in *Taxis and Toadstools*, Doubleday.

Milne, A. A., "Sand-Between-the-Toes," in *When We Were Very Young*, Dutton.

providing enrichment activities

Page 58 — Vowel digraph ai

Building Linguistic Skills

Introduction of **ai** digraph.

phoneme-
grapheme
relationships

Introduction

Write **feet** and **treat** on the chalkboard. Use them as examples to review with the children the rule that when two vowels come together in a word, usually only the long sound of the first vowel is heard. The second vowel spells no sound.

reviewing long
vowel rules

Procedure

1. Put **ai** on the board. Ask for the name of the first letter. Remind the children that the letter name is the long vowel sound. Tell the pupils that, just as in **ee** and **ea**, the second vowel in **ai** spells no sound. They will have to remember that it is there.

introducing
the **ai** digraph

Write **rain** on the board. Have the children read it. Ask someone to write **train, pain, main,** and **brain**. Have a child circle the digraph in each word and read the word.

2. Dictate the following words, having several children at the board simultaneously, and giving each a different word. (This technique keeps the group involved and alert.)

aim	air	hair	pair
tail	sail	pail	mail
paid	raid	maid	braid
bait	wait	waist	grain

3. Have the children read the following sentences as you put them on the board:

locating
the **ai** digraph

Paint the barn red.
He put a letter in the mailbox.
Her hair is in a braid.
The water went down the drain.
The train runs fast.
We can sail in the wind.
Dig a pail of sand.
Can he hammer a nail?

As each sentence is read, call on a child to circle the **ai** digraph.

4. Put **tale** and **tail** on the board and ask a child to use **tale** in a sentence. If this seems difficult, provide the sentence—for example, "I like 'The Tale of Peter Rabbit.'"—and explain the meaning of **tale**. Move on to **tail** and ask the children to use this word

in a sentence. (*Peter Rabbit has a fluffy tail.*) This is not so difficult for them. Explain that there are many words which sound like other words but mean something different and are spelled differently. Now put **sale** and **sail** under **tale** and **tail** on the board and develop the meanings in the same way. Add **hare** and **hair, bare** and **bear,** and **plane** and **plain** and follow the same procedure, using each in a simple sentence.

5. Direct the children to turn to page 58. Have each one study the list, choose a word, use it in a sentence orally, and write it on the board. Each child may call on another child to read a word and use it.

6. After most of the words have been read, those which were not chosen may be listed on the board by the teacher and read by the children. The teacher may find it necessary to explain some meanings.

7. Direct the children's attention to the purple block and the irregular word **again.** Ask the children how many vowels they see in the word. (*3.*) Ask if it looks like all the other **ai** words on the page. Explain that although it looks like the others, it is usually pronounced differently. Most people pronounce it with short *e;* only rarely is it pronounced long *a.* Call on several children to use **again** in a sentence.

8. Put the flash card for **again** with the group to be used for **ai.** Direct the children to put their hands up when they see it. Expose the cards quickly. Do not have the children read them, but have them raise their hands quickly when they see **again.** Repeat this procedure several times, changing the position of the card each time.

9. Have a short review of words with flash cards. When the children are familiar with these words to the point of rapid recognition, mix cards with **ee** and **ea** words for further word mastery.

Suggestions for Further Activities

1. Put a list of words on the board for the children to read, illustrate, and write:

train	trailer
paint	rain
sail	hair
painter	tail

2. Give the children pictures to label such as those on page 58. The children are to fill in the missing vowel digraphs: **ee, ai,** or **ea.** Duplicating Master No. 25 is similar to this exercise.

3. For writing, have the children complete these sentences. Answers may also be on the board in random order. Include two extra words with answers for better thought processes. (*gain, sail*)

Put water in a _____. (*pail*)
Hens eat _____. (*grain*)
If milk spills, it will _____. (*stain*)
The pig has a little _____. (*tail*)
If we eat fast, we get a _____. (*pain*)

Workbook page 32 follows this lesson.

Enrichment

providing enrichment activities

Stories: Lenski, Lois, *The Little Airplane,* Oxford.
　　　The Little Sail Boat, Oxford.
　　　The Little Train, Oxford.
　　Piper, Watty, *The Little Engine that Could,* Platt and Munk.

Poems: Bennett, Rowena B., "A Modern Dragon," and "Racing the Train," in *Around a Toadstool Table,* Follett.
Field, Rachel, "Rain," in *Taxis and Toadstools,* Doubleday.

poems for enrichment

Milne, A. A., "The Engineer," in *Now We Are Six,* Dutton.
Mitchell, Lucy S., "A Locomotive," in *Here and Now Story Book,* Dutton.
Tippett, James, "Trains," in *Sung Under a Silver Umbrella,* Macmillan.

58

Page 59 — A poem: An ant

Introduction

This poem has a definite rhythm and style. Read it to the class first to give them this style. The discussion motivated by the poem will probably take longer than the actual reading.

developing
a sense
of rhythm

Procedure

1. After you have read it, ask what the grass seems like to an ant; the rain puddle; the rock; a fern. If they cannot answer, have them read silently to find the answers. (*forest, sea, hill, tree*)
2. Have the group read the poem in unison; then have one or two children read it alone to the others.
3. Ask what long **e** words they can find, containing **ea** or **ee**.
4. Have other comparisons made, such as what would someone's foot seem like to the ant? an acorn? a step? What would the desk seem like to a worm? the chair to a grasshopper? Lead children to use their imaginations.

making
comparisons

Suggestions for Further Activities

Using this poem as a pattern, other original poems may be created using a variety of familiar animals, such as a toad in the garden, a snail, or a turtle.

creative
writing
of poems

Pages 60 — 61 — The Mail Carrier

carrier   deliver

Note: For use with this lesson, have on hand an envelope on which can be seen a return address, postmark, and cancelled stamp, preferably foreign.

Introduction

Begin a discussion and a free exchange on the subject of mail. Ask the children if they ever receive or send letters, invitations, magazines, etc. Ask how many ways mail is delivered, where you can mail letters, whether or not everyone has mail delivered to his home or apartment. Some children may be aware that a mail cart is used by some mail carriers. Others will not be familiar with this form of delivery. Let the children tell how their mail is delivered. Describe

developing
story
background

how you receive your mail and ask the children how mail is delivered to the school. Some children may be aware that women are employed as mail carriers as well as men.

Procedure

introducing the special words *carrier* and *deliver*

1. Have the children examine the picture that goes across the top of pages 60 and 61. Ask the children what they think the woman is doing. Ask if she is carrying the mailbag on her shoulder. Ask if someone can tell what a person is called who delivers mail. (*The children will probably say "mailman".*) Explain that the person is now called a **mail carrier.** Write the term on the chalkboard. The children should be able to decode **mail,** but will need help to read **carrier** since they have not had the i spelling of long **e.**

Have the children say the word after you several times; then have them say the phrase.

2. Add to the phrase so that the children can read it in a sentence such as: *A mail carrier delivers mail.* Assist the children to decode the special word **deliver.** The long e in the first syllable is irregular and will need to be explained. Recall for the children words they have studied such as **he, me,** and **we** in which /ē/ is represented by the single letter **e.** After the children have read the word aloud several times, ask for sentences using the words **deliver, delivers,** or **delivered.** You might hand a child an envelope with the instruction, "Deliver this to the Principal." Ask what other word could have been used instead of **deliver.** (*take, give*)

3. Use the special words in a variety of settings in sentences such as the following. Put them on the board for the children to read.

It is fun to help the mail carrier.
Gail will help deliver it.
Has the mail carrier been here?
Please help deliver this letter.

Guiding Reading for Comprehension

Allow time for silent reading of page 60. Ask questions such as:

1. What are the names of the two girls? (*Gail, Kate*)
2. What did the mail carrier tell them? (*that she needed help*)
3. Does the story tell the name of the mail carrier? (*no*)

After the children have responded, have them continue to read silently to find out how the girls helped and why the mail carrier was finding it hard to deliver the mail fast. Ask a child to read the sentence that tells what would help. (*having the numbers painted again*)

Have the entire page 61 read for better understanding of the story.

Page 62 — The Mail Carrier
(continued)

Preparation for Reading

Ask the children to scan the page and help you make a list on the chalkboard of all the words that contain **ai**. List each word even though it is repeated in the text. Ask why **Spain** and **Main** begin with capital letters. Ask which is the name of a country and which is the name of a street. Then ask the children to help you make a list of all the words that have **ee**. Write the numeral 15 on the chalkboard. Ask a child to read the two sentences aloud in which the number appears.

listing **ai** and **ee** words

Guiding Reading for Comprehension

1. Ask a child to read the first sentence. Ask how the mail carrier knew that the letter was from Spain. (*stamp, postmark, return address*) Show the children the envelope with the cancelled foreign stamp. If there is a map or globe available, point out where the letter was mailed from.
2. Have the children read the remainder of page 62 silently. When most have finished, ask what problem the mail carrier had. (*couldn't locate 15 Main Street*) Ask what the girls suggested. (*that they could help find it*)

Page 63 — The Mail Carrier
(conclusion)

Preparation for Reading

Have the children skim the page to locate any additional words that can be added to the list of **ai** words made for page 62. (*trailer, praised, again*)

Discuss the illustration of the trailer park and where mail is delivered for those who live there. Discuss the purpose of the red flag on each mailbox. (*Raised flag indicates there is mail to be picked up.*)

Guiding Reading for Comprehension

checking comprehension

After the children have read the page silently, ask them where Frank Green lived. (*Trailer number 15 in a trailer park on Main Street.*) Ask the children what it means that the mail carrier **praised** Gail and Kate. Have several children suggest what the mail carrier might have said to the girls.

Have several children share in reading the story aloud without further interruption.

Concluding the Story

discussion of jobs open to women

If it has not been discussed previously, after the story has been read, ask the children if they ever saw a woman mail carrier, bus driver, police officer, or crossing guard. Help them to see that jobs they might want to do when they grow up are possible now for men or women. Name a man teacher the children will know, and call attention to jobs such as his that once were thought to be typically feminine positions but are now held by both men and women.

Suggestions for Further Activities

exercises for independent work

1. Have the children select a caption for a picture from those listed below, draw a picture, and write the caption below their drawing.

I deliver milk.	a letter to mail
I deliver mail.	a trailer
I painted.	a train
It rained.	a pail of snails

2. Ask each child to draw the shape of a large envelope, or provide each child with a piece of paper the shape of a legal-size envelope. Dictate the following for each child to write:

Frank Green
15 Main Street
(your city)

3. Encourage the children to bring envelopes with cancelled stamps on them. These may be used to create an interesting bulletin board or used in other creative ways in the classroom.

4. Invite a small group of children to act out the story. A chair could be substituted for a mail cart.

5. From your file or from magazines have the children select pictures of workers. Ask them to make up a short story about the worker and dictate it to you.

6. Page 33 in the workbook follows this lesson.

7. Number 26 of the Duplicating Masters can be used here.

8. S*U*P*E*R Books No. 35 and 36 follow this lesson.

Enrichment

Any of the books in the *I Want to Be* _____ series, published by Children's Press are appropriate here. They can be read to the group or left for the children to look at and read if they are able to do so.

Page 64 — Recognition of long i, I, and ie

Building Linguistic Skills

Introduction of long **i**, using signal **e**, and the **ie** digraph.

introducing the
long i phoneme

Procedure

1. Make a game of changing words:

Tim	___	time
kit	___	kite
rid	___	ride
pin	___	pine
spin	___	spine

Have the class read the words as you build them, either on the board or by adding **e** to flash cards.

2. Change **mill** to **mile** and **still** to **stile**, and ask what change the children have noticed. Ask for volunteers to write **till** and then change it to **tile**; similarly change **pill** to **pile**, and **fill** to **file**. Before going on to the next spelling change, be sure that all the children understand that when the terminal letter is **e** and the vowel is long, we do not double the consonant. You may put a few words in context on the board as further drill:

changing
words with
short i to words
with long i

> The mill is a mile down the street.
> The pill made me feel better.
> Put the dimes in a pile.
> I will fill the file with letters.

Have the children read each sentence as you write it. After all the sentences are on the board, have the children underline the long **i** words.

3. Use the same steps as suggested above to bring out changes in spelling from **Dick** to **dike**, **lick** to **like**, and **pick** to **pike**. Have the children spell or write:

Mike   hike   bike   spike   strike

Note: It may be necessary to explain again that **k** without **c** is used with a signal **e**.

4. Put **dine** on the board; after the children have read it, add **r**, and again have the children read it. Do this with **fine, line, ripe, wide, time, bite, smile, ride,** and **mine.** Call attention to the sound of the **er**, showing that when there is only one consonant before the **er**, the **e** is usually serving two purposes: it is also a signal **e** to tell you that the words have a long **i**.

adding er
to words with
long i

63

5. Use many words in short phrases for rapid word recognition, fluency, and understanding. Here are some suggestions:

mine is red	bite the meat	hide the bike
a pine tree	all my life	ripe plums
a fine mill	a black line	a pile of grass
ride in a car	at his side	strike the ball

Note: With most average or above average groups, the rules taught here give enough power for decoding other words. However, with slower groups, it may be necessary to provide more visual exercises, either with flash cards or with words in context. Here are additional phrases.

ride a bike	a big spike
here is mine	inside the barn
a pile of sticks	cost a dime
a bite of apple	nine miles
a fine kite	the bride smiles

building
discrimination
of long i and
short i words

Workbook page 34 can be used here.

6. It is suggested that this be the beginning of a new lesson. Explain to the children that some words do not follow the rules. We cannot tell that they have long **i** just by looking at them. One has to try saying it with a short **i** and a long **i** to see which makes sense in the phrase or sentence. Put **find** on the board. Call on a child to read it. If he pronounces **find** with short **i**, ask if the child knows what it means. Ask if anyone has heard such a word. If not, suggest the child try a long **i**. He will recognize **find** immediately. Continue by writing **kind, him, mind, bind, sip, behind,** and **pilot** on the chalkboard. Ask the children to read each word silently twice, once with short **i** and once with long **i**, then, when you give a signal, say the word aloud as they think it should be pronounced.

Write *I will wind my top.* on the chalkboard and have the children read it. Then write *The wind fills the sails.* The pupils should become aware that only by reading the word in context can anyone identify the vowel sound. Ask the pupils to find and circle each word that contains /ī/.

The man is blind.	Bind the dog's hind leg.
Find it for her.	Look behind the desk.
The pilot is in his seat.	He is kind to me.

7. It is recommended that the next group of words be taught in a new lesson. Recall the vowel digraph rule as you put the following sentence on the board: *I can see the pie.* Ask a child to find the word that contains /ī/ and draw a circle around the letters that represent that sound. Continue this procedure with the following sentences:

1. See my green **tie.**
2. Fran will **lie** in the sun.
3. Ted hit his arm and **cried.**
4. Frank **dried** his mitt.

5. Tom **fried** the clams.
6. We **tried** to see the plane.

7. The plant will **die.**
8. Dan **tried** to **lie.**

8. Ask the children to turn to page 64. Have them read all the words aloud in one color block at a time. Help them realize that all the words in the yellow and green blocks have long i with signal **e.** In the purple block, the letter i represents long i by itself. In the blue block, long i is represented by **ie.**

variant
spellings
of long i

Suggestions for Further Activities

1. The following list can be copied by the children. They may mark the i either long or short. Marks may be diacritical, or words labeled l and s.

exercises for
independent
work

| win | s | time | l | pie | liner |
| skin | | fine | | pin | stick |

2. Play a game with the words in each color block. Tell the children to look at the words in the yellow block while you give them a clue about one of the words. Tell them you are thinking of a numeral that comes after eight, a boy's name, something you smoke, etc. Let a child tell you the word you are thinking of or have him write it on the chalkboard. If this is too difficult, use only one line of words at a time, having the children cover all lines below the line you are giving clues for.

3. Put the following list on the board or duplicate it for the children to use independently. Ask the children to change each word so that it will contain long i. Explain that in some words this will mean they will add signal **e,** such as changing **pin** to **pine.** In other words, they will need to drop a consonant before they add signal **e.**

| pin | mill | dim | rip |
| kit | pill | till | bit |

Duplicating Master No. 27 follows this lesson.
Workbook pages 35 and 36 follow this lesson.

Page 65 — Words having ir and ire

Building Linguistic Skills

Phoneme resulting from r following i; the change when signal **e** is added to **ir.**

phoneme-
grapheme
relationships

Introduction

introducing the
ir pattern

Write these words on the board or show the children pictures you have labeled: **girl, bird, fir, first grade.** Say the words and have the children repeat them after you.

Procedure

1. Ask what sound the children heard in every word or picture label. /ir/ Then ask what two letters they see in every label. (*i, r*) Tell the children that in these words, the **r** changes the **i**; it is not long **i** nor short **i** but like the ending **er.**

2. Have the children frame in each word the two letters that represent the /er/. If the words are on the chalkboard, let the children draw circles around the letters that represent /er/ in each word.

3. Develop the remaining words in this group from the known words, i.e.:

fir	___	firm
fir	___	sir
fir	___	dirt, etc.

introducing the
ire pattern

4. Recall the function of signal **e;** put **fir** on the board, add **e,** and have the children apply the signal **e** rule and read the word. Do the same with **sir.**

clarifying
word meanings

5. Direct the children to open their books to page 65. Have them pronounce all the words. Clarify the meanings by having the children use the words in sentences. If there are any words which are not understood, take the time to use them in sentences and explain their meanings. A simple explanation is enough. For example: **sire** is a word that was used many years ago when someone spoke to a king, or a servant spoke to his master. A **spire** is a tall part of a building, like a church steeple. **Tire** has two meanings: a tire for a car, and to feel tired.

6. Have the children close their books; supply them with paper. Dictate the words in random order. After the children have had time to write the words, choose a child to write his words on the board. Guide the children in checking their own work.

Suggestions for Further Activities

developing
creative writing
skills

Many easy words have been taught, and the children who do manuscript writing should be encouraged now to take simple stories of two or three sentences from dictation. They should also begin to create their own stories, using capital letters, periods, and question marks.

Easy picture books with accompanying short stories can be compiled for a class-sharing activity. Unlearned words used in the story can be spelled by the teacher. Many children will be able to read

66

them in context. Original sentences, like: *I like to swim in the summer,* or *I like to play ball,* lend themselves to good illustrations.

Nonsense jingles can also be fun. They can be dictated or originated by the children. The teacher can give the first line and have the children create the rhyming one, as:

composing
nonsense
jingles

> "I saw a tiny mouse,
> He ran into my house."

The teacher may wish to use a variety of techniques for these jingles. They are amusing to illustrate and give good opportunities for class sharing. Some oral suggestions for first lines are:

"A wee little cat _____"   "A tiny green bug _____"
"My furry little pup _____"   "A little gray mole _____"
"The funny fat pig _____"   "A busy old rat _____"

Suggestions for Further Activities

Workbook page 37 follows this lesson.
Duplicating Master No. 28 also follows.

Page 65 — Time for Bed

Introduction

Discuss the picture; then encourage the children to relate similar personal experiences. It is usually necessary to insist that the children speak loudly enough for all the class to hear. Children have a tendency to talk just to the teacher. This picture lends itself to a storytelling time. As the children relate personal experiences, they should use complete sentences and correct grammar, should speak in a pleasant voice, and should organize their thoughts. However, it is not a good idea to interrupt the children to correct errors. Often repeating the sentence after a child, directing it to the whole group, and merely using corrected grammar, teaches by usage without calling attention to the child's error.

Guiding Reading for Comprehension

Direct attention to the title. This title does not tell who is in the story. Point out that the title is short, not a whole sentence, and tells what the story is about. After silent reading, have the title read aloud.

The first sentence tells who the boys are. Have the children find the names. (*Bill and Mike*) Give even the slowest children time to read silently this two-line sentence. Then have it read aloud.

Have the children find who is talking in the next two sentences. (*Bill*) After silent reading, ask a child to read the words that Bill said just as he thinks Bill said them. Ask, "Who says he will be in bed first?"

Page 66 — Time for Bed (*continued*)

Guiding Reading for Comprehension

checking comprehension

Have the children find the word that describes how Mike put out the lamp. (*snapped*) Ask how many parts they hear in *snapped*. (Have them clap their hands if necessary.)

Ask what kind of bed Bill and Mike had. (*fine*) Find other words that describe the bed. (*big, wide*)

locating the **ai** digraph

The last sentence is a difficult one. Have the children pick out the *ai* vowel digraph words (*raised, pair*), study, and read them. Guide them in working out these words before the entire sentence is read orally. Note that here is another word (raised) that has an *ed* ending, but we hear only the *d*. Have the entire page reread before going on to the next page.

Pages 67 and 68 — Time for Bed (*continued*)

do

Introduction

drawing conclusions from picture clues

In discussing this picture, let the children draw their own conclusions as to who the man is—whether he is the father of either of the boys, a friendly policeman checking on the boys' safety, a next door neighbor, etc. Discuss the emotional reactions of the boys—scared, frightened. Discourage the use of *sad*; some children classify anything not happy as sad.

Guiding Reading for Comprehension

locating vowel sounds in the story

Have the children study the first four sentences, putting their fingers on the words as you direct them. Instruct them to find a word with a long **e**. (*see*) Find a word with a long **i**. (*hide*) Find a two-syllable word. (*under, blanket*) Find a word with a vowel digraph or long **a**. (*hair*) If they point out **afraid**, some children may read it in context; however, it may also be developed linguistically. Cover the **a**, and have the children discover the second syllable. Then allow them to see the whole word. Ask what **a** "says" as a word. (*short u*) Explain that it often has the same sound at the beginning of a word because it is not stressed **u fraid**. Have the last sentence read aloud.

Have the children read the first sentence on page 68 to find out what the boys did.

Special Word do

introducing the special word *do*

Continue the silent reading to learn what Mike told Bill to do. Have the word *do* identified, as this word is used out of order for the sake of the story. Have the thought unit read aloud (three sentences). Have the last thought unit read silently, and then have the entire page read aloud for fluency and continuity.

Pages 69 and 70 — Time for Bed
(*conclusion*)

Guiding Reading for Comprehension

checking comprehension

Ask the children to find out who speaks first on page 69. (*the man*) Ask them to find the word that tells how he talked. (*cried*) Point out that this means excitement. What did Mike and Bill do? (*ran from the tent*) Who was the man? (*Farmer Tom*) Who saw him first? (*Bill*) (Page 70) Have a child read aloud the sentence that tells what Farmer Tom had with him. (*spade*) What did he do with the spade? (*dug and tossed dirt*) Ask what Bill thought about Farmer Tom, and why. (*fine, came in time,* etc.)

oral reading for expression

Reread the story for continuity. There are several quotations in this story. Encourage good expression by telling the children to say the words just as they think Farmer Tom or Bill or Mike did.

Use this opportunity to discuss safety, fire prevention, and the need for adult supervision. Several excellent safety lessons can be initiated at the conclusion of this story.

Workbook page 38 follows this lesson.

Duplicating Masters Nos. 29 and 30 also may be used.

S*U*P*E*R Book No. 37, *Mike and the Red Suspenders*, follows this lesson.

Page 71 — Long o

Building Linguistic Skills

Introduction of long o in (1) two letter words, (2) words with signal **e,** and (3) words with long o followed by two consonants. Introduction of words not having long **o,** but with similar grapheme pattern.

Introduction

Review the signal **e** rule, again using the children's names—long and short. Tell a story about a little **mole** who ran into a **hole.** He found himself **alone,** with **no** one around; so he decided he'd **poke** his **nose** here and there until he'd made a new **home.** Put the dark-type words on the board as you talk.

Procedure

1. After the words have been put on the board, ask the children to find any words they recognize. (The children may recognize several words.) Repeat the word after the child, and ask what sound the **o** makes. Review the list; this time the children should be able to read all the words.

2. Point out that **go, so,** and **no** do not have a signal **e,** but if we were to try to say these words with a short **o,** they would not "make sense."

3. List the following words on the board and have the children read them: **sole, lone, pole, home, tone.** Use more words from the text if necessary to teach the children to recognize the long **o** sound easily.

4. To develop the irregular words, *come, some,* and *done,* use the following procedure.

a) Put the following sentence on the board:

I will come home alone.

Have the children read silently; then ask if any of the words are difficult. Some children may point to **come.** If so, ask them to try the long sound; "does it make sense?" "Try the short sound—does it make sense? This is an irregular word with a special sound. What word would be missing if you read the remainder of the sentence?" (Cover **come** with your hand and call on a child to read: I will _____ home alone.) Obtain **come** as the response to the question. Put several phrases on the board:

come here
he can come

come again
come to me

b) Follow a similar procedure to teach **some**. A suggested sentence is: *Here are some stones.*

c) A similar procedure should follow to introduce **done**: *Is my cake done?* or *Has Tom done his tasks?*

d) Flash cards with these three words should be interspersed with long **o** (signal **e**) words for rapid recognition.

5. The introduction of vowels made long when followed by two consonants can be the beginning of a new lesson if in the teacher's judgment steps 1 to 4 are enough for one lesson. Explain that some long **o** words do not require a signal **e**. Use the words in context:

recognizing long **o** words without signal **e**

Dan has the most fun at ball games.

Have the children study silently, read aloud, and then mark the long **o**. Here are suggested sentences for several of the words used in the text:

The colt did not leave the mare's side.
A man is a host in his home.
Will you hold my rope?
The gun is in a holster.

Duplicating Master No. 31 can be used here. The pictures represented are:

exercises for independent work

rose	kite	cake
gate	cone	pipe
dime	home	cape

Duplicating Master No. 32 also follows this lesson. Workbook pages 39, 40, and 41 can be used here.

Page 72 — Words having or and ore

Introduction

In introducing the **or** words with signal **e**, you should have little difficulty in getting the children to read the words directly from the text. If any of these words presents a problem, discuss and present one on the board—"My cut finger is **sore**."

introducing **or** words with signal **e**

Procedure

Explain that most words with **or** have a spelling without signal **e**, as:

I want cake **for** supper.
I need a **fork** to eat it.
It is Ned's **or** Tom's.

Use the board if necessary to present the words in context; otherwise, turn to page 72 to have the children read the lists of words. Have the children use the words in sentences if there is a difficult meaning. If the children do not recognize the meaning of such words as **lord** and **corral,** you should tell them.

Suggestions for Further Activities

1. To correlate reading and writing have the children copy the following list, supplying long or short marks: (You may prefer to have the children use L and S rather than the diacritical marks — and ◡.)

sob	hole	post	home
lock	toss	hot	bond
tone	robe		

2. Have the children select, from page 72, eight (or any number designated) words which they can illustrate. Be sure they label the pictures.

3. Put simple but interesting sentences on the board to be illustrated. Examples:

The smoke rose behind the tent.
The cork will bob on the water.
The cow hand has a rope on his saddle.
The corn is ripe now.
The robe has some roses on it.
The man stole a horse.
The mail carrier has a letter for me.

Let the children choose the ones they wish to illustrate. You may assign one, two, or even four, but they should not be expected to do more than that. Additional assignments will often result only in poor work habits.

Duplicating Master No. 33 follows this lesson.

Workbook pages 42 and 43 may be used here.

Enrichment

Poem: Milne, A. A., "Jonathan Jo," in *When We Were Very Young*, Dutton.

Page 73 — A poem: A Little Elf

Introduction

Allow the children time to enjoy the illustration. If possible, show them an acorn cap so that they can appreciate the size of the elf. Discuss various names for such little creatures—elves, brownies, fairies, etc.

enjoying the illustration

Special Word *by*

Call the children's attention to the special word in the red box. Explain that sometimes y spells long **i**. Pronounce **by** for them and have the children say it after you as they look carefully at the word. Write these phrases on the chalkboard. Ask the children to read them and to use them in sentences.

introducing the special word *by*

sit by me   by the tree   by himself

Erase **by** in each phrase; then have a volunteer replace the word in each phrase. If desired, dictate the phrases and have children write them on the chalkboard.

Procedure

1. Have the children read the poem silently. Ask them to point out words that give difficulty.
2. Ask for pairs of rhyming words.
3. Ask what words have long **o** sounds. (*alone, acorn,* and *home* are included although *acorn* is properly pronounced ā'côrn.)
4. Have the group read the poem in unison.
5. Have several children read it alone for pleasure. Stress fluency and rhythm.

reading with rhythm

Duplicating Masters Nos. 34 and 35 follow this lesson.

Page 74 — The Lost Cow

Introduction

A discussion of the pictures will bring out that the story is about a cowboy, his horse, his holster, and his gun. "Where do you think the cowboy is going? Why does he need a rope?" (*to rope calves or strays*) "—a gun and holster?" (*to shoot those animals, snakes, or*

developing story background

wildcats which might attack his cattle) "—a cowboy hat?" (*to protect him from the sun, wind, and rain; to hold food; to dip water from a creek; to use in many ways*).

Guiding Reading for Comprehension

As the children study the title ask what the story is about. Ask, "Does this tell us a little about where the cowboy may be going? What word tells what has happened to the cow?" (*lost*) Discuss again the characteristics of a good title.

Direct the children to find out what the cowboy's name is, (*Carlos Calero*) and where he is going. (*into the hills*) Have them read the first two sentences silently and aloud.

finding vowel sounds in the story

The fourth paragraph is long and difficult. It will require analysis—what are the long a words? (*braided, nail, take, taken*) What is the long e word? (*he*) What two-syllable words do you see? (*braided, corral, saddle, taken, wanted*) If the children have difficulty with "corral," ask the name of the fenced-in yard where the cowboys keep their horses. Have the class find and point to **corral**. Following the study, have the sentence read orally. With the last sentence, give an opportunity for silent reading; then ask, "For what is the cowboy going to use his rope?" (*to rope the lost cow*)

Have the entire page read aloud. Work for fluency in reading the two-line sentences.

Page 75 — The Lost Cow (*continued*)

Introduction

Discuss the picture and the tracks around the water hole. What kind of tracks might they be?

Guiding Reading for Comprehension

checking comprehension

Direct the children to read the first complete thought unit silently (two sentences). Ask whose tracks Carlos saw. (*his cow's*) Direct the class to the next thought unit (two sentences). After silent reading, ask, "Why is Carlos eager to find his cow soon?" (*wants to find her before dark*)

Ask the children to find an **or** word in the next sentence. (*more*) After silent reading, ask, "What is around the water hole?" (*sand and wet grass*) Have the children complete the page silently. Ask, "Does Carlos think he can find his cow?" (*yes*) "Why?" (*because of the tracks*) Have the entire page read orally. Turn immediately to page 76 to keep the story moving.

Page 76 — The Lost Cow
(continued)

Introduction

my

Ask the children what they think this man is doing with Carlos' cow. What clues can they get from the way Carlos is riding and from what Carlos has in his hand? (*Carlos is riding fast and has his rope ready.*)

Special Word *my*

Help the children recall that sometimes y spells /ī/. Write **by** on the chalkboard and have the children read it aloud. Ask someone to change **by** to **my**. Have a few pupils contribute sentences using **my**. Have the children turn to page 76, and scan the page for the word **my**. Ask a child who has located it to read the sentence for the group.

introducing
the word **my**

Guiding Reading for Comprehension

The page should present very few difficulties. If, however, the children hesitate over words with signal **e**, review this concept in **rode, stole,** and **rope.** It might help the children to point out that **rode** is related to **ride,** and **stole** is related to **steal.**

After the children have read the page silently, ask what the man did with Carlos' cow. (*stole it*) Ask the children how they think Carlos is planning to get the cow back. (*rope it*) Have the page read aloud.

Page 77 — The Lost Cow (conclusion)

Introduction

Here, the picture reveals the outcome of the story. Turn the children's attention immediately to the story and discuss the picture after the reading.

Guiding Reading for Comprehension

Ask which word tells how Carlos spoke to the man. (*cried*) See if the children can recall where this word was used previously. (*Time for Bed,* page 69) Then ask, "What other word tells almost the same thing?" (*called*) In this type of guided reading, the child reads

reading
to answer
specific
questions

to the point where he finds the answer. After the question has
been answered, the teacher gives another question, and the children
continue their silent reading. Here are suggested questions:

What did Carlos do with his rope? (*spun*)

How did it go through the air? (*sailed*)

What two words (in the fourth sentence) have long **o's**? (*hope, rope*)

Where will Carlos go next? (*home*)

What word describes the man? (*bad*)

Did Carlos get his cow? What did he use? (*rope*)

Discuss the duties of cowboys, such as branding, repairing
fences, feeding the cattle in the winter, and many other duties
which do not relate to "bad men," rustling, etc. Numerous stories,
including the "Cowboy Sam" series, bring out the interesting and
varied life of the cowboy.

Suggestions for Further Activities

1. Many illustrations may be created directly from the cowboy
discussion. If this story is used to motivate a regular art lesson, a
colorful bulletin board or display can be made with crayoned pictures on 12″ x 18″ paper, cut colored construction paper on 12″
x 18″ paper, or tempera paint on 18″ x 24″ paper.

2. Use rhyming exercises and correlate them with writing. Put

a list of words on the board, and then put a rhyming list in random
order beside it. Have the children copy the lists and draw a line
from each word in the first column to the one that rhymes in the
second:

nose	sail
smoke	wide
hail	rose
ride	seed
feed	poke

3. The following list of words may be given to the children
either on the board or on a mimeographed sheet. Direct the children to supply a rhyming word for each. In some cases, it will be
necessary to allow the children to use their books for reference:

alone	————	cork	————
sail	————	most	————
tree	————	mind	————
horn	————	rake	————

Workbook page 44 is a comprehension check of the story. Workbook page 45 is similar to exercises 2 and 3 above.

Enrichment

Stories: Lenski, Lois, *Cowboy Small,* Oxford.

Chandler, Edna W., "Billy and the Cowboys," in the *Cowboy Sam* series, Beckley-Cardy.

Poems: Roberts, Elizabeth Madox, "Milking Time," in *Sung Under the Silver Umbrella,* Macmillan.

Stevenson, R. L., "The Cow," in *A Child's Garden of Verses,* Oxford.

providing enrichment activities

Page 78 — Vowel digraphs oa and oe

Introduction

> does

· Review the pattern of two vowels coming together and tell the children that this new group of vowels (or digraphs) will make it possible for them to read many new words.

phoneme-grapheme relationships

At all times, remember that almost without exception first-grade children have a strong desire to learn to read. This desire, plus pride in their own reading ability, provides intrinsic motivation which is better than most artificial devices. Your enthusiasm as the children show success will carry the pace of your lesson. You must show outward enthusiasm for little children. This is contagious. If you react to their growth in reading, they will appreciate the importance of what they are accomplishing.

developing enthusiasm for reading

Procedure

1. Put **oa** on the board, or, if you wish, turn directly to the text. Have the children "guess" the sound. As soon as it has been established as long **o**, go immediately into word recognition. This should not be difficult since the words present little difficulty either in spelling or in meaning.

introducing the oa and oe digraphs

2. Explain that **oe** spells the same sound as **oa** and have the children read the words in the book.

3. **Does** is a special word. Have the children look at it and say what they think it is. Ask if they know any word like that. Have they ever heard such a word? Put the following sentence on the board: *Ned does not like milk.* Have the children read it silently; then ask if anyone thinks he can read the sentence. After a child has read it aloud, point to **does** and call on a child to say the word. Be sure all the children see and hear the word. Put *Does Ann like milk?* on the board and have the children read it silently. Then have a child read it aloud. Call on a child to frame **does**. Explain

teaching the special word does

that this is spelled like the **oe** words but has an exceptional pronunciation.

playing a rapid recognition game

4. Play a short game for rapid recognition, either with word cards or in any drill form that you have found profitable, so that the children do not spend time painfully sounding out words. Establishing the phoneme-grapheme pattern thoroughly should result in rapid recognition. Always allow the child to think through the word silently; then, when he pronounces it, he should be able to say it as a whole. Do not encourage "sounding out" aloud, and never have them pronounce the initial sound without the following vowel sound.

Suggestions for Further Activities

exercises for independent work

1. Many of these words are easily illustrated. Put on the board sentences that require more detail in the pictures than has been suggested previously, for example:

> A toad is in the road.
> The oars are in the boat.
> The goat eats grain.
> Put some soap in the water.

building creative writing skills: nonsense jingles

2. Have the children write jingles which can also be illustrated and made up into a book. The teacher may begin by giving a first line or asking the children to give a sentence ending with one of the words from the page. Example: *He put on his coat.* Then have the children create the second line. It can be nonsense. This is fun for everyone.

> "He put on his coat
> And jumped in the boat."

The children can copy several jingles from the board for practice in writing and then make their own books. Some are included on page 48 of the workbook.

3. Give the children mimeographed sheets with the first lines and part of the second lines. They must supply the last word as suggested in the previous game. Include the words from this page.

Duplicating Master No. 36 follows this lesson.
Workbook pages 46, 47, and 48 also follow this lesson.
S*U*P*E*R Book No. 38, *The Real Bandit,* can be used here.

Enrichment

providing enrichment activities

Stories: Burgess, Thornton W., *The Adventures of Old Mr. Toad,* Little.

Poems: Bennett, R. B., "Boats," in *Around a Toadstool Table,* Follett.

Rossetti, Christina, "The Bridge," in *Sing Song,* Macmillan.

Pages 79 and 80 — The Sad Goat

Introduction

once

A brief discussion of the picture may serve to introduce the story. However, the title will elicit more curiosity about what is going to happen than the illustration. Have the children discover the title and read to find out why the goat is sad.

using the title to motivate reading

Guiding Reading for Comprehension

Note that this story introduces the full paragraph with sentences starting anywhere on a line. In guiding the children, have them recognize the capital letter as the beginning and the period as the end of the sentence. As you explain about the capital letter and the period (or question mark, etc.), use the word "sentence" and tell the children that a sentence tells a complete thought. It is about something, and tells what that something did. Give a few examples of phrases and sentences aloud, such as, "the little red wagon." Ask, "What is this about?" (*little red wagon* or *wagon*) "What did it do?" (*It doesn't tell.*) Say, "The little red wagon rolled down the hill," and discuss the subject and the action. Several phrases may be put on the board either before or after the oral reading to give further experiences with a complete sentence. The children read and notice that the phrases are not complete. You may have to ask, "What did it do? What happened to it?" to complete them. Here are some suggestions:

introducing the full paragraph

understanding sentence structure

> My red car _____
> Mother's green dress _____
> Ned's little boat _____

Work for fluency in phrasing and correct intonation at the end of the sentences.

Call the children's attention to the first phrase (four words) and have someone read these words aloud. Since the special word **once** may be unfamiliar to children in the group, the teacher may have to read the phrase, "once upon a time." Put **once** on the board, and add a flash card to those which the children are using for further review.

introducing the special word once

Ask what kind of story this is going to be. (*fairy story, make-believe,* etc.) Have them find the **oa** words in the first paragraph. As a child finds a word, he may write it on the board. Have the children read these words. Ask, "What words describe the goat?" (*old, fat*) Continue the study of the second paragraph by asking, "What does the goat want to do?" (*hop like a toad*)

On page 80, ask who is talking in the first paragraph. (*oak tree*) Ask, "Does he think the goat will be able to hop? (*no*) Does he think

checking comprehension

anything can hop? (*yes, a frog*) How can you tell now that this is really a make-believe story?" (*the animals and the tree talk*) The time taken in discussion of true and untrue stories is rich and well spent. This story is the first of this kind.

oral reading
with
expression

Have the pages read aloud; stress expression. Have one child "be" the goat, one the tree, and one the narrator. Perhaps "playing" the story will lead to other animal plays.

Page 81 — The Sad Goat (*continued*)

Introduction

enjoying the
humor

Let the children enjoy the humor of the picture before getting to the words. They will be eager to continue the story.

Guiding Reading for Comprehension

Ask the children to find a word in the first paragraph which means the same as **hop.** (*leap*) Continue silent reading with as few questions as possible.

Have the children read page 81 silently to learn what happened to the goat.

dramatic
reading
of the story

Have the pages read aloud for fun. Perhaps children will want to "play" out the whole story. Let many children take the parts to sustain interest.

Did the goat learn a lesson? This story could lead into the reading of some of the simple fables, like "The Fox and the Grapes."

Suggestions for Further Activities

creative
writing activity

1. The logical activity here would be a study of the fables, or an opportunity for creative stories involving things that talk. Encourage the children to tell stories (three sentences) having an animal or an inanimate object talk—*a house, a boat, a tree,* etc. Some of these stories may be recorded by the teacher for a class book, a writing lesson, or a drawing lesson.

developing
discrimination
of nouns and
verbs

2. A worksheet activity can be included here to help the children become aware of things they can see or touch, and things they can do. This is the beginning of a recognition of nouns and verbs using the meaning of a noun or verb rather than its grammatical term. Give the children a worksheet similar to the following one. Have the children cut off the words and paste them under the correct heading according to whether they are names of things or action words.

See	Do
run	swim
skip	make
boat	spin
doll	grass
cake	goat

Duplicating Master No. 37 follows this lesson.
Workbook pages 49 and 50 also follow.

Enrichment

Include, as well as the fables mentioned below, some of the simple stories with talking characters.

Stories and Tales: *Aesop's Fables,* from the Translation of Thomas James and George Tyler Townsend, Lippincott.

Crampton, Gertrude, *Scuffy, the Tug Boat,* Golden Press.

Piper, Watty, *The Little Engine That Could,* Platt and Munk.

Wiggin, Mrs. Kate Douglas, and Smith, Nora Archibald, *Talking Beasts, A Book of Fable Wisdom,* Doubleday.

providing
fables for
enrichment

81

Page 82 — Introduction of j

Building Linguistic Skills

Recognition of **j** and addition of words having this letter to vocabulary.

Introduction

Have the children say some of the familiar Mother Goose rhymes with you. Include "Jack be Nimble" and "Jack and Jill." Read or teach "Jonathan Jo" from A. A. Milne's *When We Were Very Young*. After the children have recited and enjoyed the poems, list the names of the people on the board: *Jack, Jill,* and *Jonathan Jo.*

Procedure

1. Have the children say each name after you. Continue with the following list:

jump	just	jam
jet	Jenny	jar
jelly	Jean	jug

2. Ask the children for words beginning with /j/. List them on the board. If the children give words that begin with soft **g** (gentle), explain that in some words **g** spells the same sound. List these words separately.

3. Ask the following questions; all answers must begin like **Jack:**

The name of a very fast airplane. (*jet*)
Something which holds pickles, or jelly, or peanut butter. (*jar*)
A story which makes us laugh. (*joke*)
The name of a month. (*June, January, July*)
Another word for leap. (*jump*)

4. Provide practice in auditory discrimination. Ask the children to listen for words that begin with /j/. Give instructions as to how the class is to respond.

car	move	Bob	Jill	lamb	saw
run	jump	Joe	Peg	jam	say
jeep	run	Tom	Nan	ham	jaw

5. Dictate words either for board work or for written work at the seats. Here is a suggested list:

jet	jug	Jim
job	jerk	Jack
just	jab	Jan
jump	joke	Jill

Choose words from the text. Check the work with the children immediately. This can be done by having a child put the correct spelling on the board after all have finished.

6. Present the words on page 82, with discussion, illustration, and sample sentences. Many words may have to be used by you in sentences. For example:

To be fair means to be *just.*
Just also means exact, or exactly.
"This tastes *just* right."
"The judge gave him a *just* punishment."

Don't *jog* my elbow when I am writing.
We *jogged* along in the pony cart.

The logs were so closely packed, they couldn't be moved in the river. We call this a *jam.*
Sometimes the paper gets *jammed* in the machine (typewriter, etc.).
Strawberry *jam* is sweet and sticky and good on toast.

The rubbish we throw out is *junk.* A type of Chinese sailboat is a *junk.*

Suggestions for Further Activities

1. Mimeograph simple riddles. Have each child choose the correct answer from a group of words and write it on the line.

I am good to eat. I am sweet. I am often red. I am _____. jot jug just jam	I am made of glass. I hold jam. I am a _____. jet jug jar jump
I am a name. I am not a girl's name. I am like bed. I am _____. Jean Jed Jack Jim	I am a name. I am a girl's name. I am like moan. I am _____. Jean Jill Joan Jed

83

These riddles are similar to the workbook, page 53.

2. Put words on the board, omitting vowels. Allow the children to use their books and complete a real word:

j__b   j__g   j__st
j__nk   j__rk   j__ke

playing the "Jack" game

3. Play the "Jack" game. Answers to all the questions must begin with *Jack.*

Who fell down the hill? (*Jack and Jill*)
Who sat in a corner and ate pie? (*Jack Horner*)
What gives us light at Halloween? (*Jack-o'-lantern*)
Who jumped out of a box? (*Jack-in-the-box*)
Who paints your windows at night? (*Jack Frost*)

Duplicating Master No. 38 follows this lesson.
Workbook pages 51, 52, and 53 follow this lesson.

providing
enrichment
activities

Enrichment

Poems: A. A. Milne, "Jonathan Jo," in *When We Were Very Young*, Dutton.
Laura Richards, "The Baby Goes to Boston," in Arbuthnot, *Time for Poetry*, Scott, Foresman.

Page 83 — Ride in a Jet Plane

using personal
experiences
as story
background

Introduction

A discussion of the picture will include reading the name of the plane and discussing it. Time should be provided here for personal experience stories.

Guiding Reading for Comprehension

Have the title read; then have the children find the name of the boy. (*Jack*) Ask these questions after the children have read the paragraph silently: "Where was he going? Had he ever been in a plane before?" (*West Falls, no*)

checking
comprehension

Guide the children to read the description of a jet plane in the second paragraph and finish the page silently. Have the children find the descriptive words in the paragraph. (*big, sleek*) Have the page read aloud.

84

Page 84 — Ride in a Jet Plane (*continued*)

Guiding Reading for Comprehension

Guide the children in silent reading. Have them point to any words they do not know. List these words on the board and have the children help each other. Some may have difficulty with **pilot** and **beside**. Analyze these words. If no child has difficulty, put each word on the board and ask a child to read it. Be sure that all the children are ready for silent reading.

guiding silent reading

Check comprehension with questions such as: "What safety device do the boys have?" (*seat belts*) "What is the pilot's job?" (*run the Star Fire*) "What is the hostess' job?" (*serve the passengers*)

Have the page read aloud. Watch for any labored "sounding." If this is apparent, use Word Recognition cards during a practice period.

avoiding elaborate sounding

Pages 85 and 86 — Ride in a Jet Plane (*conclusion*)

Guiding Reading for Comprehension

Have the children read to answer a question for each paragraph. Work for *rapid* silent reading.

developing speed in silent reading

Suggested questions: "How can Jack move the back of his seat?" (*press a button*) "What did the hostess bring? (*dinner*) What else can the boys do on the plane?" (*read, sleep*) "Was the Star Fire early, late, or on time?" (*on time*) "Who met Jack at the airport?" (*Jan*) "How did he get to Jan's home?" (*jeep*) "Did Jack like his ride on the jet?" (*yes*) Have the page read aloud; then have the entire story reread.

A discussion of airplane travel is the logical conclusion of the story.

Suggestions for Further Activities

1. Inaugurate flash card games between small groups with a pupil leader, or allow the children to use flash cards in pairs, checking each other. Be sure that **j** words are included with the cards.

exercises for independent work

2. Further practice in sentence recognition can be included here. Give the children a worksheet of phrases and sentences. They will read each one and determine whether it is a sentence or phrase. They may put a period at the end of each sentence and leave a

phrase with no mark at the end. Here are some suggestions for phrases and sentences:

Jack rode in his big red car
The sleek jet plane
Jean can jump and run
Jack and Jill
Ned will kick the ball
He can run fast
Once I
A jar of jam
We lost the oar
The fat old toad

Duplicating Master No. 39 duplicates this exercise.

Workbook page 54 may be used following this lesson and is a comprehension check of the story. Workbook page 55 gives further practice with sentence structure.

Enrichment

Stories: Gramatky, Hardy, *Loopy,* Putnam's.
Lenski, Lois, *The Little Airplane,* Oxford.
Phleger, Frederick, *Ann Can Fly,* Random.
Whitehouse, *Real Book of Airplanes,* Doubleday.

Poems: Green, Mary M., "Aeroplane," in Arbuthnot, *Time for Poetry,* Scott, Foresman.
Tippett, James, "Up in the Air," in Arbuthnot, *Time for Poetry,* Scott, Foresman.

Page 87 — Introduction of v

Building Linguistic Skills

v in the initial, medial, and terminal position and the addition of these words to the reading vocabulary.

Introduction

Cut out a large red heart and write a small and large **v** on it. Hold it up and say, "This is a *valentine.*" Have the children repeat *valentine.* Be sure that the children are putting an **n** sound at the end of the word, and not an **m** sound.

Procedure

1. Follow this activity with the list below, having the children place the teeth firmly on the lower lip and exaggerate the sound:

voice	victrola	vacant
violet	victory	very
violin	vaccination	vinegar

2. Have the children identify words beginning with **v** in the following list. The response can be any action the teacher chooses. (Note that these words have been selected for fine auditory discrimination. Enunciate them very clearly):

went	fairy	vouch	foal	vigor
vent	leery	pouch	volt	wiggle
find	very	found	fork	finger

<blockquote>building auditory discrimination of initial **v** phoneme</blockquote>

3. Have the children hear **v** as a terminal sound. Have them say **stove, love, give, have, dive, cove, rave,** and **move.**

4. Have the children repeat the following words: **Rover, Dover, cover, over, waving,** and **diving.** Ask where they hear the **v.** (*middle*)

5. Say, *"A vest has no sleeves."* Ask which word started with **v.** Put it on the board. Continue, saying the sentences aloud as you put on the board the words that start with **v.**

We vote for our president.
A van is a big truck.
A vow is a promise.

<blockquote>medial and terminal **v** phonemes</blockquote>

Have the children draw a line around all the **v's** in the words listed on the board.

6. Say, *"My dog's name is Rover."* Put *Rover* on the board and have the children draw a line around the **v.** Continue with other sentences, always listing the word with **v** on the board and having the children mark that letter:

a) He is a good *diver.*
b) Are you *saving* your money?
c) We swam in the *river.*
d) My ring is made of *silver.*
e) Does this pan *have* a *cover?*
f) The light is *over* the *stove.*
g) The *driver* wore *gloves.*
h) We will *move* to a new house.

<blockquote>building visual discrimination of the **v** grapheme</blockquote>

7. Call attention to the irregular word **have** and ask if the children notice anything strange about this word. If no child notices the short **a** sound with the signal **e**, recall the signal **e** rule; then ask what vowel sound they hear in **have.**

8. On a separate part of the board, list these irregular words to be reviewed. Deal with them one at a time. **Live, give, river,** and

<blockquote>teaching the irregular word *have*</blockquote>

87

reviewing
irregular words

liver can be treated like **have.** You can recall the others by reviewing the first list to see whether the children can detect the irregular pronunciations. If they do not hear the unusual **o** in **move** and **gloves,** it will be necessary to point it out. The irregular words **love, glove** and **dove** can be developed separately until the children are familiar with them. Flash cards should be used to develop and review this vocabulary.

developing
word
meanings

9. Some words, such as **vacant, eave, pave,** and **vent,** may be unfamiliar to the children, or may present some difficulty. It will be necessary to put these words on the board and develop their meaning with the children.

10. The final step in all these lessons should be a dictation of the words for written work either at the board or at the children's desks. Check the words after this lesson, so that the children can see their errors, as well as seeing the correct form.

Suggestions for Further Activities

exercises for
independent
work

1. List words on the board, including some special words, and have the children draw a line around the long and underline the short vowels:

vote	dive	vent	hive	five
liver	cave	have	stove	over

If you have been using the diacritical marks — and ⌣, they can be used here.

2. Give the children a duplicated sheet similar to the following, or use Duplicating Master No. 40.

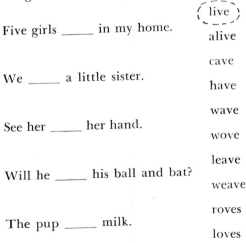

using new
words in
sentences

Five girls _____ in my home.

We _____ a little sister.

See her _____ her hand.

Will he _____ his ball and bat?

The pup _____ milk.

(live)
alive
cave
have
wave
wove
leave
weave
roves
loves

3. Give the children a list of words with the vowel missing; have them write a complete word:

88

```
st__ve        v__n         l__ve
w__ve         v__st        d__ve
sl__ver       v__te        g__ve
p__ve         v__lt        m__ve
```

Workbook pages 56, 57, and 58 follow this lesson.

Pages 88 and 89 — Van's Cave

Introduction

A full discussion of the illustration should precede the reading of
this story. This man may be considered a hermit or a recluse—not
a "bad man."

Guiding Reading for Comprehension

After the title has been read, have the children study the page
and be ready to answer questions. Ask, "What furniture has Van?"
(*bed, stove*) "What are the bed and stove made of?" (*old lumber
and old bricks*) "What is the dog's name?" (*Spot*) "Does he like this
home?" (*yes*) "Why?" (*It is home.*) Have the page read aloud. It
should be read by more than one child unless the class reads very
easily by now.

Ask who knows the first word on page 89. (*once*) Recall the word
once. Guide the reading of the second sentence by asking what one
calls a group of ducks. After getting the answer, ask what word
tells that Van shot his gun. (*fired*) Ask how many parts they hear
in *fired* (*1*).

Have the children read to find out what Van told Spot to do.
(*Jump into the water*) Direct them to finish the page silently. Ask
what word tells how Spot got into the water (*jumped*) and what
they will do with the ducks. (*eat*) Continue with oral reading. Suggest that they continue the story to see whether Van and Spot enjoyed their duck dinner.

Page 90 — Van's Cave (*conclusion*)

Introduction

Have the children look at the illustration on page 90. Guide their
observation by questions such as:

89

What animal is going away from the cave? (*a wolf*)
What does it have in its mouth? (*a duck*)
Do you see the other four? What do you think happened to them?

What was Van busy doing? (*building a fire*)
On page 90, what was Spot doing? (*sleeping*)
What should he have been doing? (*guarding the ducks*)
What would have made Spot tired? (*five trips in the water*)
Who had a meal of five ducks? (*the wolf*)
What else might he have done with them?
What do you think Spot will do next time?

Guiding Reading for Comprehension

Ask the children to read page 90 silently. List on the board any words that they indicate are difficult. Go over the list with the group. It is probable that **leave, lies, near,** and **roast** will need to be reviewed.

To check comprehension, ask for volunteers to be the wolf, Spot, and Van. Have them go through the actions they learned about from the picture and from reading the page. Have "Van" read his lines directly from the book. Have the others follow the action.

Ask the children to return to page 88 and read the entire story aloud without interruption.

Workbook pages 59, 60, 61, and the tests on pages 62 to 64 follow this lesson.

S*U*P*E*R Books No. 39 and 40 can be used here.

Enrichment

Stories: All stories about "things that go" are excellent.
Burton, Virginia, *Choo Choo, Katy and the Big Snow, Mike Mulligan and His Steam Shovel,* **Houghton.**
Freeman, Lydia, *Chuggy and the Blue Caboose,* **Viking.**

Poems: Field, Rachel, "Taxis," in *Taxis and Toadstools,* Doubleday.

Games for Review

Any games or devices used here for review will serve doubly if the teacher strives for fluency in phrase reading and speed in word recognition. It is fun to put phrases or sentences on the board; give the children an opportunity to read them silently and aloud, and then have them shut their eyes. Erase one word, say "Open" and see who can tell which word is gone. That child may erase another word, and so the game continues until nearly all the words have been erased.

Put some of the more difficult words in a box (*mailbox*). A child may choose a "letter." If he can read the word he has chosen, he may keep the word until all the words have been chosen. Have the children count to see who received the largest number of letters. This game may also be played by choosing a mail carrier who carries words in a sack. As he walks around, the child either reaches in and draws a word or he is given one by the mail carrier. Play as the above game.

Line up some chairs one behind the other. As the children give the correct response to the exposed flash card, they can ride on the "train."

Play "Jump the Brook," placing four or five flash cards on the floor 2′ or 3′ apart. A child reads a card, jumps over it to the next; reads it, and so on until he has safely jumped each brook. If he fails a word, he gets his feet wet—the teacher says the word and the child repeats it. He continues, then, to the other words. It is most important to remember that failure on a word should not deny him the opportunity to read the other words.

Some commercial games that are favorites with children can be adapted and used as word games, such as Dominoes, Old Maids, or Bingo.

Word-O is an example of how Bingo can be adapted to review and reinforce vocabulary. On heavy cardboard, make six cards similar to the two examples below. Each card must contain the same words but in a different arrangement. One set of **Word-O** cards could review long **o** and long **a** words, another set could review **k**, **c**, and **ck** words. The cards below review the sixteen special words presented in Book B.

her	said	for	I
been	do	once	by
puts	of	were	does
to	deliver	my	carrier

were	carrier	does	of
by	puts	her	been
I	said	for	deliver
to	do	my	once

To play **Word-O,** you will also need to prepare 16 smaller cards, approximately 2″ by 3″ on which you can print the special words, and a supply of small colored markers such as small squares of colored paper.

Choose a child to be the reader and give him the stack of sixteen small word cards. Distribute the larger word cards to individual children. As the reader calls out a word, each child should cover that word on his card with one of the small colored markers. Have the reader continue to call out one word at a time, placing each card face down as he reads it. The first child to get a row of markers across, down, or diagonally, shouts "Word-O".

When the child calls "Word-O" the other children should keep their markers in place while the teacher checks the winner's card by having him uncover his words one at a time, and saying the words aloud. In case an error has been made, the game can continue until someone wins.

Tests for Book B

Evaluation or Check Sheet *
Beginning and Ending Consonant Sounds and Medial Vowel Sounds

This test should help the teacher evaluate each pupil and prepare a plan for future teaching. Give each child a copy of the chart on page 93. Say each word once. Have the child draw a line around the correct letter that represents the beginning sound. Repeat the word. Ask the child to draw a line around the letter that represents the middle sound (the vowel sound). Say the word a third time. Ask the child to draw a line around the letter that correctly represents the ending sound.

Dictate the following words:

1. just	5. cot	9. win
2. step	6. lend	10. sad
3. mark	7. bug	
4. trip	8. torn	

* This test also appears on Duplicating Master 41, Book B.

	Beginning Sound			Middle Sound (Vowel)			Ending Sound		
1.	d	j̲	v	a	e	u̲	t	p	l
2.	s̲	l	p	a	e̲	i	b	p̲	d
3.	n	m̲	v	o	a̲	u	l	k̲	d
4.	b	t̲	p	a	i̲	e	d	b	p̲
5.	c̲	j	g	o̲	a	u	j	t̲	l
6.	h	l̲	f	o	u	e̲	d̲	b	t
7.	b̲	p	g	a	o	u̲	k	g̲	h
8.	f	t̲	p	u	o̲	a	m	n̲	h
9.	w̲	v	r	a	e	i̲	h	n̲	m
10.	c	s̲	g	e	i	a̲	k	d̲	j

Test on Special Words *

The following is a test of the special words presented in Book B. Distribute duplicated copies of the test to the children. Explain that they are to look at the three words in each box as you say one word. They are to select that word and draw a line under it.

hut her ten̲	see said sled̲	been̲ over̲ for	A I Oh̲
do̲ toe̲ rule	on oven once̲	die̲ by̲ fly̲	for̲ fork̲ wolf
puts̲ pulls̲ pants	top to flew̲	were̲ stir̲ fur	oven of̲ off̲
us muss does̲	my̲ pie̲ sky	carpenter carrier cares̲	deliver̲ Delaware̲ flipper

* This Test on Special Words also appears on Book B Duplicating Master 42.

Spelling Test from Dictation

The following test covers all the sound spellings presented in Book B. If twelve would be too many for your children at one time, break the test into three parts and dictate eight words at a time in three different sessions. Inform the children when a word contains a vowel sound represented by a digraph, or when the vowel is made long by adding signal **e**.

Part I:

1.	winter	___	It snows in the winter.	___	winter
2.	barn	___	Cows are kept in the barn.	___	barn
3.	dented	___	His car is dented.	___	dented
4.	saw	___	I saw her yesterday.	___	saw
5.	lake	___	We skate on the lake.	___	lake
6.	small	___	The show is not for small children.	___	small
7.	little	___	She found a little kitten.	___	little
8.	block	___	Drive around the block.	___	block
9.	bank	___	He went into the bank.	___	bank
10.	stare	___	It is not polite to stare.	___	stare
11.	me	___	Is it for me?	___	me
12.	keep	___	May I keep the dog?	___	keep

Part II:

1.	east	___	The sun rises in the east.	___	east
2.	train	___	The train runs on a track.	___	train
3.	like	___	I like to walk in the woods.	___	like
4.	tried	___	Frank tried to beat Jim.	___	tried
5.	girl	___	A girl can be the leader.	___	girl
6.	nose	___	A cat's nose is damp.	___	nose
7.	more	___	Do you want more milk?	___	more
8.	corn	___	Corn is a tasty vegetable.	___	corn
9.	coat	___	Please hang up your coat.	___	coat
10.	goes	___	He goes past my house every day.	___	goes
11.	jaw	___	I hurt my jaw.	___	jaw
12.	five	___	Gail's sister is five.	___	five

Bibliography

ENRICHMENT MATERIAL FOR BOOK B

Collections of Stories and Poems

Aesop's Fables, from the translation of James and Townsend, Philadelphia: J. B. Lippincott Co.

Arbuthnot, May Hill, *Time for Poetry,* Chicago: Scott, Foresman and Co.

Association for Childhood Education, *Sung Under the Silver Umbrella, Told Under the Magic Umbrella,* New York: The Macmillan Co.

Bailey, Carolyn Sherwin, *Merry Tales for Children,* New York: The Platt and Munk Co., Inc.

Bennett, Rowena B., *Around a Toadstool Table,* Chicago: Follett Publishing Co.

Brown, Margaret Wise, *Country Noisy Book,* Chicago: Scott, Foresman and Co.

Burgess, Thornton W., *The Adventures of Old Mr. Toad,* Boston: Little, Brown and Co.

De Huff, Elizabeth W., *Taytay's Tales,* New York: Harcourt, Brace and Co.

Field, Rachel, *Taxis and Toadstools,* Garden City, New York: Doubleday and Co., Inc.

Hubbard, Alice and Babbitt, Adeline, *The Golden Flute,* New York: The John Day Co.

Hutchinson, Veronica, *Chimney Corner Stories,* New York: G. P. Putnam's Sons.

Milne, A. A., *Now We Are Six* and *When We Were Very Young,* New York: E. P. Dutton and Co., Inc.

Mitchell, Lucy Sprague, *Here and Now Story Book* and *Another Here and Now Story Book,* New York: E. P. Dutton and Co., Inc.

Rosetti, Christina, *Sing Song,* New York: The Macmillan Co.

Stevenson, R. L., *A Child's Garden of Verses,* New York: Oxford University Press, Inc.

Wiggin, Kate Douglas and Smith, Nora Archibald, *Talking Beasts, A Book of Fable Wisdom,* Garden City, New York: Doubleday and Co., Inc.

Stories

Anderson, C. W., *Billy and Blaze,* New York: The Macmillan Co.

Beaty, John Y., *Story Pictures of Farm Animals,* Chicago: Beckley-Cardy Co.

Beim, Jerrold and Lorraine, *Two Is a Team,* New York: Harcourt, Brace and Co.

Brown, Margaret Wise, *Baby Animals,* New York: Random House, Inc.

Burton, Virginia, *Choo Choo*, Boston: Houghton Mifflin Co.
_____, *Mike Mulligan and His Steam Shovel*, Boston: Houghton Mifflin Co.
_____, *Katy and the Big Snow*, Boston: Houghton Mifflin Co.
Chandler, Edna W., *Cowboy Andy*, and *Cowboy Sam* series, Chicago: Beckley-‑ Cardy Co.
Flack, Marjorie, *Angus and the Cat*, Garden City, New York: Doubleday and Co., Inc.
Freeman, Lydia, *Chuggy and the Blue Caboose*, New York: The Viking Press, Inc.
Gag, Wanda, *Millions of Cats*, New York: Coward-McCann, Inc.
Gramatky, Hardy, *Loopy*, New York: G. P. Putnam's Sons.
Hader, Berta and Elmer, *Cock a Doodle Doo*, New York: The Macmillan Co.
Huber, Miriam, *I Know a Story*, New York: Row, Peterson and Co.
Jackson, Kathryn and Byron, *Big Farmer Big and Little Farmer Little*, New York: Simon and Schuster, Inc.
Lenski, Lois, *Cowboy Small, The Little Airplane, The Little Farm, The Little Sailboat, The Little Train*, New York: Oxford University Press, Inc.
McCloskey, Robert, *One Morning in Maine*, New York: The Viking Press, Inc.
Meeks, Esther K., *Friendly Farm Animals*, Chicago: Follett Publishing Co.
Phleger, Frederick, *Ann Can Fly*, New York: Random House, Inc.
Piper, Watty, *The Little Engine That Could*, New York: The Platt and Munk Co., Inc.
Whitehouse, Arch, *Real Books About Airplanes*, Garden City, New York: Doubleday and Co., Inc.

Other Books

Baker, Eugene and Green, Carla, series *I Want to Be a* _____., Chicago: Children's Press, Div. Regensteiner Publishing.
Brown, Margaret Wise, *Golden Egg Book*, New York: Simon and Schuster, Inc.
_____, *Runaway Bunny*, New York: Harper and Brothers.
Crampton, Gertrude, *Scuffy the Tug Boat*, New York: Golden Press.
Dubois, William P., *Lion*, New York: The Viking Press, Inc.
Eastman, P., *Sam and the Firefly*, New York: Random House, Inc.
Freeman, Don, *Fly High, Fly Low*, New York: The Viking Press, Inc.
Geisel, Theodor (Dr. Seuss), *And To Think That I Saw It On Mulberry St.*, New York: Vanguard Press, Inc.
Guilfoile, Elizabeth, *Nobody Listens to Andrew*, Chicago: Follett Publishing Co.
Hader, Berta and Elmer, *Farmer in the Dell*, New York: The Macmillan Co.
Hoff, Syd, *Sammy, the Seal*, New York: Harper and Brothers.
Minarik, Else H., *Father Bear Comes Home, Little Bear*, New York: Harper and Brothers.
Rey, H. A., *Curious George*, Boston: Houghton Mifflin Co.
Udry, Janice M., *A Tree Is Nice*, New York: Harper and Brothers.

Record Correlation for Basic Reading

Record Code:

A E D—Phoebe James Creative Rhythms (78 RPM)
B—Bowmar (78)
C R G—Children's Record Guild (78)
G L P—Golden Record Library (33⅓)
L E—R.C.A. Adventures in Music Series (33⅓)
M S B—Musical Sound Book Records (78)
R C A E—Albums—R.C.A. Victor Basic Educational Albums (78 or 45)
Y P R—Young People's Record Guild (78)

BOOK B RECORDS

PAGE	STORY	RECORD	TITLE
10	Wags Gets Wet	CRG 1004	Little Red Wagon
29	Flat Sam	Columbia MJV 110	The Little Turtle (Burl Ives)
		LP	Yertle, the Turtle
		MSB 78010	Turtles, from Carnival of Animals, Saint-Saens
		CRG 1008	Castles in the Sand
		AED 22	Phoebe James Sea Life Rhythms
42	The Black Cow	CRG 5001	Ride 'Em Cowboy
		YPR 716	Little Cowboy
47	Black Mane and Tim	RCA E 71	Running Horses, Galloping Horses, High-Stepping Horses
51	Red Deer	RCA E 78	The Little Hunters
54	Seal	CRG 1028	I Am A Circus
65	Time for Bed	CRG 1024	Let's Be Firemen
		YPR 615	Little Firemen
74	The Lost Cow	YPR 716	The Little Cowboy
79	The Sad Goat		(See records for story on page 9)
83	Ride in a Jet Plane	YPR 706	Trains and Planes
		B Alb. B301	Rhythm Time (Mechanical Rhythms Record 1551)

Music Correlation for Basic Reading

Basic Music Series

Allyn and Bacon Co.	This is Music—2
American Book Company	American Singer 1 (2nd edition) American Singer 2 (2nd edition)
	Music for Young Americans 1 Music for Young Americans 2
Follett Publishing Co.	Together-We-Sing Series Music Round the Clock—1st Grade
Ginn and Company	Ginn, First Grade Ginn, Kindergarten
Silver Burdett Co.	Music for Early Childhood—Kindergarten Music Through the Day—1st Grade (Books of the Music for Living Series)

BOOK B SONG CORRELATION

STORY PAGE	TITLE	PAGE	SONG TITLE	MUSIC REFERENCE BOOK
2	The Cats and the Cart	90	Kitty	Music for Young Americans 1
		59	The Little Cat	Music for Early Childhood
		81	Cat and the Bird	American Singer 1 (2nd ed.)
		*23	I Love Little Pussy	Music Round the Clock
10	Wags Gets Wet	41	Little Red Wagon	Music Through the Day
		9	My Little Red Wagon	American Singer 1 (2nd ed.)
15	Ted and Rags	144	Oh Where, Oh Where	American Singer 1 (2nd ed.)
		143	Little Dog, What Do You Say?	Ginn, 1st Grade
		149	My Dog Jack	Ginn, 1st Grade
		*89	My Big Black Dog	Music for Young Americans 1
		77	Skipper	American Singer 1 (2nd ed.)
		*38	My Little Dog	Music Through the Day

* Denotes song is recorded in album that goes with series.

FILMSTRIP CORRELATIONS

Index of sources:

Cur: Curriculum Films
EBF: Encyclopaedia Britannica Films
Eye Gate: Eye Gate House
FOM: Popular Science Publishing Company
Jam Handy: The Jam Handy Organization
McG: McGraw-Hill Films
SVE: Society for Visual Education

OUR STORY	PAGE	FILMSTRIP TITLE	SOURCE
The Cats and the Cart	2	My Cat Taffy	Eye Gate
Wags Gets Wet	10	Paul's Puppy	EBF
		The Puppy	McG
		Randy Takes Care of His Dog	McG
		Our Puppy	McG
		My Dog Sandy	EBF
Ted and Rags	15	Paul's Puppy	EBF
		The Puppy	McG
A Fawn at Dawn	20	The Deer and the Haystack	SVE
		Winter Is Here	SVE
		Winter Adventures	SVE
The Cow and the Frog	24	The Biggest Frog in the World	Cur
		The Rabbits and the Frogs	McG
Flat Sam	29	The Turtles	Cur
		Terry's Turtle	EBF
		The Rabbit and the Turtle	Eye Gate
		My Turtle	Eye Gate
		The Turtle	McG
		Tubby Turtle	SVE
The Little Sled	35	Winter is Here	SVE
		Winter Adventures	SVE
The Black Cow	42	Mr. Peet, Dairy Farmer	Cur
		Cows	Cur
		Cows on the Farm	Jam Handy
		The Story of Milk	SVE
Black Mane and Tim	47	Horses on the Farm	Jam Handy
		Hoppy, the Rabbit	Jam Handy

MOTION PICTURE CORRELATIONS

Index of sources:
  Coronet: Coronet Films
  EBF: Encyclopaedia Britannica Films
  McG: McGraw-Hill Films

OUR STORY	PAGE	FILM TITLE	SOURCE
The Cats and the Cart	2	Three Little Kittens	EBF
		Kitty Cleans Up	McG
		Mittens, the Kitten	Coronet
Wags Gets Wet	10	Shep, the Farm Dog	EBF
		Tippy, the Town Dog	EBF
		Adventuring Pups	McG
Ted and Rags	15	Shep, the Farm Dog	EBF
		Tippy, the Town Dog	EBF
		Frank and His Dog	EBF
		Our Pet Show	Coronet
		Peppy, the Puppy	Coronet
		Adventuring Pups	McG
A Fawn at Dawn	20	Spotty, Story of a Fawn	Coronet
		Spotty, the Fawn in Winter	Coronet
		Mother Deer and Her Twins	EBF
		Children in Winter	EBF
		Winter Is an Adventure	Coronet
		The Seasons of the Year	Coronet
The Cow and the Frog	24	The Cow and the Sprite	Coronet
		Tad, the Frog	Coronet
		The Frog Princess	Coronet
Flat Sam	29	Hare and the Tortoise	EBF
		Tuffy, the Turtle	Coronet
		The Toad and the Turtle Race	McG
The Little Sled	35	Play in the Snow	EBF
		Children in Winter	EBF
		Winter on the Farm	EBF
The Black Cow	42	Judy Learns About Milk	McG
		Frisky, the Calf	Coronet
Black Mane and Tim	47	Pride, the Saddle Horse	EBF
		Adventures of Bunny Rabbit	EBF
		Hoppy, the Bunny	Coronet
		Sparky, the Colt	Coronet

102

Acknowledgments

Editorial Assistance by Carolyn Shoaff, New Castle, Pennsylvania.
Music Enrichment Materials by Anita E. Scott, New Castle Area Schools, Pennsylvania.
Illustrations by Carol Kitzmiller and Ann Atene.

BOOK B
BASIC READING

GLENN McCRACKEN
New Castle, Pennsylvania

CHARLES C. WALCUTT
Queens College, Flushing, New York

J. B. LIPPINCOTT COMPANY
PHILADELPHIA, NEW YORK

25.749.1

CONTENTS

ar

arm	darn	tar	dart	tart	cart
art	card	mar	hard	harm	part
star	car	farm	far	scarf	
are					

The Cats and the Cart

Tom is a farm hand.
Tom has a farm cart.

A card is on the cart.
Tom puts eggs in his cart.

puts

2

Tom runs off to get a tart.
Tom is far from the cart.

The cats are at the cart.
to

3

Can the cats harm the eggs?
The cats harm the eggs.
And the eggs harm the cats.

er

fast	faster	start	starter
tend	tender	hunt	hunter
wet	wetter	camp	camper
farm	farmer	mend	mender
her			

5

ed

hand	handed	mend	mended
start	started	hunt	hunted
dent	dented	dart	darted

into upon after across under garden

ed

farm farmed

harm harmed   darn darned

7

ed

camp	camped	stop	stopped
cross	crossed	snap	snapped
stamp	stamped	miss	missed
gasp	gasped	toss	tossed

8

w W

wet went wig wag win
winter west western wagon
water want wasp was
were

9

Wags Gets Wet

Wags, the dog, got into the wagon.
It was a red wagon.

The wagon started to run fast.
Faster and faster it went.

Pam darted after it.
Topper, the cat, ran after Pam.

Pam wanted to stop the wagon.
Wags must not get harmed.

The wagon stopped at the pond.
Wags did not stop.

Into the water went Wags!
Pam darted in after him.

Pam and Wags got wet.
Wags was not harmed.

The red wagon hit hard.
It was dented.

w   W

war   wart   warm   swarm

Ted and Rags

Rags ran into the water.
The water was warm.

Ted wanted to run in the water.
Ted did not want to get wet.
Rags got wetter and wetter.

"Get it, Rags, get it," said Ted.
"Get the gun in the water."

Rags went to get the gun.
Rags got wetter and wetter.
said

Rags got the gun for Ted.
Ted went to Rags to get it.

Rags was wet.
Rags got the water off.
for

The water went from him to Ted.
The water was on Ted.

"The water is wet," said Ted.
"The water is wet and warm."

18

aw

saw   paw   raw   caw

draw   dawn   fawn

A Fawn at Dawn

Sam handed Win a gun.
Win handed Sam a dart.

Sam and Win went into the forest.
Fawns were in the forest.

20

At dawn, Win saw a fat fawn.
The fawn saw Sam and Win.

It started to run fast.
It ran into a winter camp tent.

Sam and Win hunted for the fawn.
It hid in the tent.

Sam started to the farm.
Sam must not harm a fawn.

Win and Sam went to the farm.
Win wanted to get warm.

The raw winter dug into his hands.
Win and Sam did not harm the fawn.

OW

how   now   cow   down   town

The Cow and the Frog

A fat frog sat on a raft.

A tan cow saw the fat frog.

The cow sat down on the raft.

Down, down went the raft.
It went down into the water.

Now the cow sits in the water.
The frog sits on the cow.

25

l L

lot	lad	log	lap		let	letter
lip	last	less	lamp		list	lost

clan	class	clap	clod	clam	slip
sled	slap	slit	slop	slam	glad
flat	flag	flip	flop	plot	plug
plan	plant	held	help	helmet	antler

ll

all   tall   fall   call   hall   stall
wall   fell   well   will   hill   till
mill   pill   sill   small   still

pull   full   pullet

Pull the full pan.
Put the water in the pot.

Ellen on a hill-top
Ellen on a hill
Ellen on a hill-top-hill
Still, still, still

Adele H. Seronde

Flat Sam

Ten small clams sat in the sand.
The clams sat under a log.
The water was still and warm.

Clams can dig in the sand.

The clams saw Flat Sam.

Flat Sam wanted to get the clams.

A clam called,

"Dig, clams, dig!

Get under the sand!

Dig far into the sand!"

Flat Sam swam after the clams.

The clams dug and dug in the sand.

Will Flat Sam get the clams?

Flat Sam swam fast to the log.

Slap, slap went the water.
Flat Sam did not get the clams.

The small clams were in the sand.
The small clams had dug far down.

b B

ban	bat	bar	bad	Ben	best
bed	big	bin	bid	beg	bond
but	bug	bog	bit	barn	belt
bass	bet	bag	bald	bull	bun
ball		bend		bump	bent

rob	rub	rib	tub	cob	cub
hub	slab	stub	dab	cab	crab
stab		bib		bulb	Bob	Tab

bled blimp blot brim brag number

le

bottle   little   apple   rattle

puddle   saddle

The Little Sled

Bob and Ben sat on a little sled.
The sled started to run fast.
It ran down the big hill.

Faster and faster went the sled.
Bob and Ben held on to it.
"Stop the sled!" said Bob.

The sled hit a bump.
Bob and Ben fell from the sled.

The little sled did not stop.
It ran on and on.
It ran into a red barn.

The barn bent the little sled.
And the sled dented the barn.

Bob and Ben got wet.

k   K

kit   kill   kept   kiss   kid   keg
milk   silk   task   mask   risk   brisk
kin   dark   lark   park   bark   mark
ask   kilt   kitten

37

Mitten, mitten
   A mitten on a cat.
Kitten, kitten
   A kitten on a mat.

Adele H. Seronde

ck

rack	sack	tack	pack	lack	back
neck	deck	peck	nick	sick	tick
pick	wick	lick	mock	rock	sock

dock	lock	duck	luck	bucket	stack
stick	block	stuck	pluck	smack	snack
black	track	truck	trick	flock	kick

The Little Black Dog

Pick up a stick
And hit the ball —
Hit it across the park.
The little black dog
Will run and run,
And get the ball back and bark!

nk

rank	tank	sink	ink	pink
sank	bank	drink	rink	mink
Frank	drank	sunk	link	wink
blanket				

The Black Cow

Bob has a black cow.
The cow is kept in a barn.
Bob rubs her back and neck.
The cow will not harm Bob.

42

Bob wants to get milk.
Bob can milk his black cow.

Tab is a tan cat.
The cat begs for a drink of milk.
Bob milks the cow for Tab.
of

a-e

can	cane	mat	mate
at	ate	fat	fate
rat	rate	man	mane
cap	cape	pan	pane

care

ar   are

car	care		bar	bare
mar	mare		star	stare
far	fare		scar	scare

dare	hare	ware	flare

45

a-e

name late Kate safe base bake
tale date blame make sake lake
taste same came wake made spade

gale bale stale take sale hate
gate state grate game pale cake
plane tame skate rake snake

Black Mane and Tim

Black Mane was a pet mare.
Her mane was black as slate.

Tim was a small, brown hare.

Black Mane and Tim ate grass.

47

Tim saw a snake in the grass.
The snake came up to Tim.
Tim saw the snake stare at him.
It was a big, black snake.

Black Mane ran to the gate.
Tim was on her back.
Tim made Black Mane run fast.
"Run, Black Mane, run!" said Tim.

Black Mane came to the gate.
It was as tall as the mare.
"Help, Tim!" said Black Mane.

Tim helped Black Mane.
Black Mane helped Tim.
The snake did not get the hare.

e   E   ee

he   be   me   we   Pete   here

bee   see   seem   seed   seek   steel
flee   beet   beef   meet   deer   reel
deep   keep   peek   peel   feel   tree

feed   feet   need   sleep   week   street
deeper   feeler   keeper   fifteen   green
been

Red Deer

Red Deer went to a beet farm.

He wanted to feed on the beets.

The deer did not see the farmer.

The farmer did not want Red Deer
to nip the tops off his beets.

The beet farmer hid under a tree.

He had a stick.

The farmer picked up the stick
and started after Red Deer.

Red Deer ran down a steep hill.
He hid in the deep grass.
But the farmer saw his antlers.

Red Deer swam
across the deep water.

He ran into the tall trees.

The farmer did not hit him.

Red Deer will not be back
to the beet farm.

He will not nip the tops
off the beets.

He will feed in the forest and
be safe from the farmer.

ea

ear	bean	leak	meat	reap	neat
eat	fear	lean	pea	seam	read

east	feast	leap	peak	seat	near
ease	heat	lease	tea	bead	beak
beat	heal	least	seal	team	please

beam	leaf	meal	rear	tease	beard
beast	lead	mean	sea	dear	pleat
repeat	retreat		steam		defeat

Don and Nell Dig Clams

Don and Nell went to the sea to dig clams.

Nell wanted clams to eat.

Don had a bucket and a rake on the end of a stick.

He and Nell dug for clams.

"We will steam the clams," said Don.

"I will heat the water," said Nell.

Don and Nell steamed the bucket of clams.

I

"Please pass me a clam," said
Nell.

Nell ate ten clams for her meal.
Don ate fifteen clams.

After the big meal, Don and
Nell were full of clams.

ai

aim claim rain gain main grain
drain brain train faint maid paid
braid fail rail hail mail tail
Gail raise waist

air hair pair

sail pain Spain gait slain stain
plain pail nail bait wait trailer
afraid sprain praise strain paint
again

An ant
Will pass
In a forest
Of grass
On a twig
Near a rain-
Puddle
Sea.
And a rock
Will be
A hill
Tip-top
And a fern
A monster
Tree.

Adele H. Seronde

The Mail Carrier

The town mail carrier said, "I need help to deliver the mail."

"I can help," said Gail.

"Please, can I help?" asked Kate.

carrier   deliver

Gail held her cap. Kate put her
hand on the mail cart.

The mail carrier said, "It's hard
to deliver the mail fast. Lots of
numbers are hard to see. The
numbers need to be painted
again."

"Here is a letter from Spain," said the mail carrier.

"It is for Frank Green. The address is 15 Main Street. But I did not see a number fifteen on Main Street."

"I can help," said Kate.

"Let me help, too," said Gail.

"Frank Green is in a trailer on Main Street. His trailer is number fifteen in the trailer park."

The mail carrier praised Gail and Kate and said, "Please help me again."

i   I   ie

mine ride pile Mike bite spike
pine side bike tile dime strike
nine hide time like pipe spite

fine wide life stile smile bride
line ripe mile lime stride diner
kite wife spine dike crime finer

find kind mind bind behind pilot

tie lie die pie cried dried tried

ir

sir   fir   first   bird   girl   dirt

sire   fire   spire   hire   tire

Time for Bed

It is time for Bill and Mike to be in bed.

"I like to be in bed at nine," said Bill.

"I will be in bed first."

Mike snapped off the lamp.

Mike and Bill had a fine bed in a tent.

It was a big, wide bed.

It was raised on a pair of blocks.

"I see a man," cried Bill.
"Hide under the blanket.
I am afraid."

Mike and Bill hid under the red
and black blanket.

"Lie still," said Mike.

"The man cannot see us. Do not be scared."

The man saw Mike and Bill.

Mike peeked at him.

do

"Wake up, Mike," cried the man.

"The tent is on fire."

Mike and Bill ran from the tent.

Bill saw the man first.

It was Farmer Tom.

He had a spade.

He dug and tossed dirt on the fire.

"Farmer Tom is a fine man," said Bill.

"He came in time to stop the fire."

N o O o

go no so

hole mole sole lone pole home
bone cone alone stone rode robe
smoke globe hope note poke stole
rose rope dose dome lope nose
tone drone

post   most   colt   bolt   host
holster   poster   old   hold   told

come   some   done

ore   or

ore	more	core	wore
sore	bore	tore	before

or	nor	for	fork	corn
horn	born	torn	worn	cord
cork	lord	horse	acorn	corral

72

A little elf
Sat by himself
　　Alone,
Alone in the lap
Of an acorn cap
　　At home.

Adele H. Seronde

The Lost Cow

Carlos Calero rode his horse into the hills.

He went to find a lost cow.

Carlos wore a gun.

He had taken his braided rope from its nail near the corral. He had put the rope on his saddle.

He wanted to rope the lost cow and take her back home.

Carlos came to a water hole.

He saw some tracks his cow had made in the mud.

"I hope the lost cow is near," said Carlos. "I want to find her before dark."

Carlos saw more and more tracks in the sand and in the wet grass.

"Now I will find the cow," said Carlos. "Her tracks go here."

Carlos rode to the top of a big hill.

He saw a man and a cow.

"The man stole my cow," said Carlos. "I will take her from him."

Carlos started down the big hill.

He had his rope in his hand.

my

"Stop!" Carlos cried.

The man did not stop.

Carlos spun his rope in the air and made it sail at the man.

"I hope I can rope the man and the cow," he said.

Carlos got the cow in his rope.

"Now I can take the cow home," said Carlos. "The bad man will not get her."

oa

oak   oat   boat   coat   goat   soap
road   toad   soak   foam   roam   loaf
coal   goal   moan   groan   cloak   croak

oar roar soar board coarse hoarse

oe

toe   foe   hoe   woe   goes
does

The Sad Goat

Once upon a time a goat sat near the side of a road. He was an old, fat goat.

The goat saw a green toad go down the road. "I want to hop like a toad," said the fat old goat. "I want to hop, hop, hop down the road."

once

"A fat goat cannot hop," said
the oak tree. "A frog can hop
like a toad, but a fat goat cannot
hop at all."

"I can hop if I want to," said
the goat. "I will leap into the
road now."

The old goat made a big leap for a fat goat. But he did not land on the road.

"Help me!" said the goat. "Help me get down from here! I cannot hop like a toad! I hop like a fat goat."

"The goat will not boast now," said the tall oak tree. "He will not boast how far he can leap."

j   J

jet	jig	jar	jag
job	Jeff	jog	jam
just	jug	James	jerk

jump	Jess	jaw	jot
Jack	Jim	Jones	joke
Jill	Jean	jab	junk
Jan	jeep	jail	Joan

Ride in a Jet Plane

Jack went on a trip in a jet plane. It was his first plane ride. He went to see Jan. Jan's home was in West Falls.

A jet plane is big and it goes fast. It is as sleek as a bird. Jack had not seen a plane as big as the Star Fire.

The big plane sat still and Jack went up the steps.

Jack sat beside James. James smiled at Jack. Jack smiled at James.

"We must lock the seat belts," said James.

Jack and James saw the pilot in the cockpit. His job was to pilot the Star Fire. The big plane started and went up, up, up.

"See how little the cars and trucks are," said Jack.

"Press the little button and the seat will go back or forward," said James.

"Here is dinner," said the hostess.

"Dinner on a jet is fun," said James.

"Just like home!" said Jack. "We can eat, read, or sleep if we want to."

The Star Fire came to West
Falls on time. Jack ran down the
steps.

Jan came in a jeep to meet
Jack and take him home.

"I had fun on the big jet
plane," Jack told Jan.

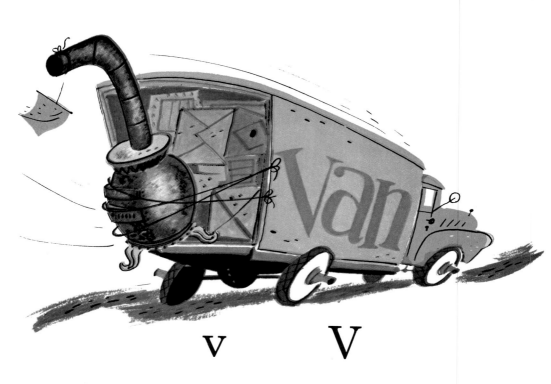

v V

van	stove	five	save
vent	alive	wave	over
vest	dive	wove	Rover
vile	gave	leave	diver
vote	pave	weave	vacant
volt	cave	cove	silver
vow	hive	eave	sliver

live	give	love	move
liver	have	glove	dove

87

Van's Cave

Van is an old, old man. He lives in a cave near a lake. Van has a bed and a stove in the cave.

Van made the bed of old lumber. He made the stove of old bricks. He sleeps in the bed. Spot likes to sleep near the stove. His bed is just an old coat.

Spot likes to live in Van's cave. It is home for the old man and the dog.

Once Van and Spot went to
hunt ducks. Van saw a flock of
ducks land on the lake. He fired
and fired at the ducks.

"I hit five ducks," said Van.
"Jump into the water, Spot, and
get the ducks for me."

Spot jumped into the waves
and swam to get the ducks.

"Fine dog," said Van. "We will
eat the five ducks."

Van and Spot went back to the
cave. Van made a fire.

Spot must not leave the ducks.
He lies down near the cave.

"The fire is hot," said Van. "I
will roast the ducks now."

Van did not see his five ducks.
And Spot was fast asleep.

"Bad dog," said Van. "Now we
must go and get more ducks."

Phoneme-grapheme Sequence in Books A – D

Book A

Sound	Page	Sound	Page	Sound	Page
short a	1	p	12	hard g	29
n	2	short i	15	hard c	32
r	3	s	18	h	36
d	5	short o	20	f	39
short u	7	t	22		
m	9	short e	25		

Book B

Sound	Page	Sound	Page	Sound	Page
ar	1	le	34	ai	58
er	5	k	37	long i, ie	64
ed	6	ck	39	ir	65
w	9	nk	41	long o	71
aw	19	signal e	44	ore, or	72
ow(cow)	24	a(care)	45	oa	78
l	26	long a	46	oe	78
ll	27	long e,ee	50	j	82
b	33	ea	54	v	87

Book C

Sound	Page	Sound	Page	Sound	Page
sh	1	-ing	33–38	dg,dge	89
ch,tch	5	-ed	44–47	-tion,-sion	97
th	8	er as er	52	oo(cook)	102
wh	14	ar as er	53	oo(food)	102
qu	17	ir,or,ur as er	54	ow(snow)	115
x	18	-y,-ay	64	ow(cow)	118
y	19	-ey	64	ou	119
z	20	soft c	75	long u	130
ng	26	soft g	88	ue,ui	130

Book D

Sound	Page	Sound	Page	Sound	Page
oi	1	kn	26	ea as long a	62
oy	1	silent b	36	ear	62
ew,eau	8	silent l	36	ie as long e	72
aw,au	14	silent g	48	ei as long e	72
ph as f	18	silent h	48	ei as long a	78
hard ch	18	silent gh	48	eigh as long a	78
ch as sh	18	gh as f	48	ey as long a	78
wr	26	ea as short e	62	ough	101

Acknowledgments

Illustrations: Ann Atene, Ruth and Allan Eitzen, Les Gray, Roland V. Shutts, Carol Wilde, and George Wilde.
Cover design: Phil Rath.